AF661915

HISTORY OF MEDIEVAL LITERATURE

P. K. Sinha
Jagdish K. Ghosh

Commonwealth

History of Medieval Literature

© Reserved

Edition : 2019

ISBN 978-81-311-0326-5

Published by :
COMMONWEALTH PUBLISHERS PVT. LTD.
4831/24, Prahlad Street,
Ansari Road, Darya Ganj,
New Delhi - 110002
Ph. : 23275511, 23257835
e-mail : commonwealthbooks@gmail.com

Laser Typesetting by :
Rishu Computers
Delhi

Printed at :
Roshan Offset Printers
Delhi

Preface

Medieval literature is a broad subject, encompassing essentially all written works available in Europe and beyond during the Middle Ages. The literature of this time was composed of religious writings as well as secular works. Just as in modern literature, it is a complex and rich field of study, from the utterly sacred to the exuberantly profane, touching all points in-between. Because of the wide range of time and place it is difficult to speak in general terms without over-simplification, and thus the literature is best characterised by its place of origin and/or language, as well as its genre.

The present book *History of Medieval Literature* offers the general reader help of every kind in understanding of medieval literature. The main focus of this book remains the lives and works of the principal authors of medieval period. The book is intended for advanced level students of literature, who are taking exams or modules in this field. It may also be suitable for teachers, researchers and the general reader who is interested in the history of literature. The breadth and accuracy of this volume will surely make it the standard reference book of its kind for years to come.

Authors

Contents

1

Introduction to Medieval Literature

The Middle Ages saw the beginnings of a rebirth in literature. Early medieval books were painstakingly hand-copied and illustrated by monks. Paper was a rarity, with vellum, made from calf's skin, and parchment, made from lamb's skin, were the media of choice for writing. Students learning to write used wooden tablets covered in green or black wax. The greatest number of books during this era were bound with plain wooden boards, or with simple tooled leather for more expensive volumes.

Wandering scholars and poets traveling to the Crusades learned of new writing styles. Courtly Love spawned a new interest in romantic prose. Troubadours sang in medieval courtyards about epic battles involving Roland, Arthur, and Charlemagne. Literature exploded from the universities as scholars began to question convention and write social commentary, as well as poetic fiction.

Language saw further development during the Middle Ages. Capital and lowercase letters were developed with rules for each. Books were treasures, rarely shown openly in a library, but rather, kept safely under lock and key. Finding someone who might loan you a book was a true friend. Some might rent out their books, while others, desperate for cash, might turn to the book as a valuable item to be pawned.

Medieval Literature is a broad subject, encompassing essentially all written works available in Europe beyond and during the Middle Ages (encompassing the one thousand years from the fall of the Western Roman Empire ca. AD 500 to the beginning of the Florentine Renaissance in the late 15th century). The literature of this time was composed of religious writings as well as secular works.

Just as in modern literature, it is a complex and rich field of study, from the utterly sacred to the exuberantly profane, touching all points in-between. Because of the wide range of time and place it is difficult to speak in general terms without oversimplification, and thus the literature is best characterised by its place of origin and/or language, as well as its genre.

Medieval Languages

Since Latin was the language of the Roman Catholic Church, which dominated Western and Central Europe, and since the Church was virtually the only source of education, Latin was a common language for Medieval writings, even in some parts of Europe that were never Romanised. However, in Eastern Europe, the influence of the Eastern Roman Empire and the Eastern Orthodox Church made Greek and Old Church Slavonic the dominant written languages.

The common people continued to use their respective vernaculars. A few examples, such as the Old English *Beowulf,* the Middle High German

Nibelungenlied, the Medieval Greek Digenis Acritas and the Old French *Chanson de Roland,* are well known to this day. Although the extant versions of these epics are generally considered the works of individual (but anonymous) poets, there is no doubt that they are based on their peoples' older oral traditions. Celtic traditions have survived in the lais of Marie de France, the *Mabinogion* and the Arthurian cycles.

Anonymity

A notable amount of medieval literature is anonymous. This is not only due to the lack of documents from a period, but also due to an interpretation of author's role that differs considerably from the romantic interpretation of the term in use today. Medieval authors were often overawed by the classical writers and the Church Fathers and tended to re-tell and embellish stories they had heard or read rather than invent new stories. And even when they did, they often claimed to be handing down something from an auctor instead. From this point of view, the names of the individual authors seemed much less important, and therefore many important works were never attributed to any specific person.

Religious Works

Theological works were the dominant form of literature typically found in libraries during the Middle Ages. Catholic clerics were the intellectual center of society in the Middle Ages, and it is their literature that was produced in the greatest quantity.

Countless hymns survive from this time period (both liturgical and paraliturgical). The liturgy itself was not in fixed form, and numerous competing missals set out individual conceptions of the order of the mass. Religious scholars such as Anselm of Canterbury, Thomas Aquinas, and Pierre Abélard wrote lengthy theological and philosophical treatises, often attempting to reconcile the teachings of the Greek and Roman pagan authors with the doctrines of the Church. Hagiographies, or "lives of the saints", were also frequently written, as an encouragement to the devout and a warning to others.

The *Golden Legend* of Jacobus de Voragine reached such popularity that, in its time, it was reportedly read more often than the Bible. Francis of Assisi was a prolific poet, and his Franciscan followers frequently wrote poetry themselves as an expression of their piety. *Dies Irae* and *Stabat Mater* are two of the most powerful Latin poems on religious subjects. Goliardic poetry (four-line stansas of satiric verse) was an art form used by some clerics to express dissent. The only widespread religious writing that was not produced by clerics were the mystery plays: growing out of simple tableaux re-enactments of a single Biblical scene, each mystery play became its village's expression of the key events in the Bible. The text of these plays was often controlled by local guilds, and mystery plays would be performed regularly on set feast-days, often lasting all day long and into the night.

During the Middle Ages, the Jewish population of Europe also produced a number of outstanding writers. Maimonides, born in Cordoba, Spain, and Rashi, born in Troyes, France, are two of the best-known and most influential of these Jewish authors.

Secular Literature

Secular literature in this period was not produced in

equal quantity as religious literature, but much has survived and we possess today a rich corpus. The subject of "courtly love" became important in the 11th century, especially in the Romance languages (in the French, Spanish, Provençal, Galician-Portuguese and Catalan languages, most notably) and Greek, where the traveling singers—troubadours—made a living from their songs. The writings of the troubadours are often associated with unrequited longing, but this is not entirely accurate (aubade, for instance). In Germany, the Minnesänger continued the tradition of the troubadours.

In addition to epic poems in the Germanic tradition (e.g. *Beowulf* and *Nibelungenlied*), epic poems in the tradition of the *chanson de geste* (e.g. *The Song of Roland & Digenis Acritas*) which deal with the Matter of France and the Acritic songs respectively, courtly romances in the tradition of the *roman courtois* which deal with the Matter of Britain and the Matter of Rome achieved great and lasting popularity. The *roman courtois* is distinguished from the *chanson de geste* not only by its subject matter, but also by its emphasis on love and chivalry rather than acts of war.

Political poetry was written also, especially towards the end of this period, and the goliardic form saw use by secular writers as well as clerics. Travel literature was highly popular in the Middle Ages, as fantastic accounts of far-off lands (frequently embellished or entirely false) entertained a society that, in most cases, limited people to the area in which they were born. (But note the importance of pilgrimages, especially to Santiago de Compostela, in medieval times, also witnessed by the prominence of Geoffrey Chaucer's Canterbury Tales.)

Women's Literature

While it is true that women in the medieval period were never accorded full equality with men (although some sects, such as the Cathars, afforded women greater status and rights), some women were able to use their skill with the written word to gain renown. Religious writing was the easiest avenue—women who would later be canonised as saints frequently published their reflections, revelations, and prayers. Much of what is known about women in the Middle Ages is known from the works of nuns such as Clare of Assisi, Bridget of Sweden, and Catherine of Siena.

Frequently, however, the religious perspectives of women were held to be unorthodox by those in power, and the mystical visions of such authors as Julian of Norwich and Hildegard of Bingen provide insight into a part of the medieval experience less comfortable for the institutions that ruled Europe at the time. Women wrote influential texts in the secular realm as well—reflections on courtly love and society by Marie de France and Christine de Pizan continue to be studied for their glimpses of medieval society.

Midelval Allegory

Allegory in the Middle Ages was a vital element in the synthesis of Biblical and Classical traditions into what would become recognizable as Medieval culture. People of the Middle Ages consciously drew from the cultural legacies of the ancient world in shaping their institutions and ideas, and so allegory in Medieval literature and Medieval art was a prime mover for the synthesis and transformational continuity between the ancient world and the "new" Christian world. People of the Middle Ages did not see the same break between themselves and their classical predecessors that modern observers see; rather, they saw continuity with themselves and the ancient world, using allegory as a synthesizing agent that brings together a whole image.

Four Senses of Scripture (Ways of Interpreting Scripture) There were four senses in which scripture was interpreted in the Middle Ages. Literal, typological, moral and anagogical. There were four categories of allegory used in the Middle Ages, which had originated with the Bible commentators of the early Christian era. The first is simply the *literal* interpretation of the events of the story for historical purposes with no underlying meaning. The second is called *typological,* which connects the events of the Old Testament with the New Testament; in particular drawing allegorical connections between the events of Christ's life with the stories of the Old Testament. The third is *moral* (or *tropological*), which is how one should act in the present; the "moral of the story". The fourth type of allegory is *anagogical,* dealing with the spiritual or mystical as it relates to future events of Christian history, heaven, hell, the last judgment; it deals with prophecies.

Thus the four types of allegory deal with past events (literal), the connection of past events with the present (typology), present events (moral), and the future (anagogical).

Dante describes the four meanings, or senses, of allegory in his epistle to Cangrande della Scala. He says the allegories of his work are not simple, but:

"Rather, it may be called "polysemous", that is, of many senses [allegories]. A first sense derives from the letters themselves, and a second from the things signified by the letters. We call the first sense "literal" sense, the second the "allegorical", or "moral" or "anagogical". To clarify this method of treatment, consider this verse: *When Israel went out of Egypt, the house of Jacob from a barbarous people: Judea was made his sanctuary, Israel his dominion* (Psalm 114).

Now if we examine the letters alone, the exodus of the children of Israel from Egypt in the time of Moses is signified; in the typological sense, our redemption accomplished through Christ; in the moral sense, the conversion of the soul from the grief and misery of sin to the state of grace; in the anagogical sense, the exodus of the holy soul from slavery of this corruption to the freedom of eternal glory.. they can all be called allegorical. "

Medieval allegory began as a Christian method for synthesizing the discrepancies between the Old Testament and the New Testament. While both testaments were studied and seen as equally divinely inspired by God, the Old Testament contained discontinuities for Christians — for example the Jewish kosher laws.

The Old Testament was therefore seen in relation to how it would predict the events of the New Testament, in particular how the events of the Old Testament related to the events of Christ's life. The events of the Old Testament were seen as part of the story, with the events of Christ's life bringing these stories to a full conclusion. The technical name for seeing the New Testament in the Old is called *typology*.

One example of typology is the story of Jonah and the whale from the Old Testament. Medieval allegorical interpretation of this story is that it prefigures Christ's burial, with the stomach of the whale as Christ's tomb. Jonah was eventually freed from the whale after three days, so did Christ rise from his tomb after three days. Thus, whenever one finds an allusion to Jonah in Medieval art or literature, it is usually an allegory for the burial and resurrection of Christ. Another common typological allegory is with the four major Old testament prophets Isaiah, Jeremiah, Ezekiel, and Daniel. These four prophets prefigure the four Apostles Matthew, Mark, Luke and John. There was no end to the number of analogies that commentators could find between stories of the Old Testament and the New.

There also existed a tradition in the Middle Ages of *mythography*—the allegorical interpretation of pagan myths. Virgil's *Aeneid* and Ovid's *Metamorphoses* were standard textbooks throughout the Middle Ages, and each had a long tradition of allegorical interpretation. An illustrative example can be found in Siena in a painting of Christ on the cross. At the top of the cross can be seen a bird pecking its own breast, blood pouring forth from the wound and feeding its waiting chicks below. This is the pelican whose "story" was told by the Roman naturalist Pliny the Elder. Thus by analogy to a "pagan" source, Christ feeds his own children with his own blood.

Allegory was even seen in the natural world, as animals, plants, and even non-living things were interpreted in books called bestiaries as symbols of Biblical figures and morals. For example, in one bestiary stags are compared to people devoted to the Church, because (according to medieval zoology) they leave their pastures for other (heavenly) pastures, and when they come to broad rivers (sin) they form in line and each rests its head on the haunches of the next (supporting each other by example and good works), speeding across the waters together.

Before the 5th century the traditions of allegorical interpretations were created in a time when rhetorical training was common, when the classics of mythology were still standard teaching texts, when the Greek and Roman pantheon of Gods were still visible forms (if not always fully recognized by the more learned populace), and when the new religions such as Christianity adopted or rejected pagan elements by way of allegoresis.

It was in this period that the first pure, freestanding allegorical work, called *Psychomachia* ("Soul-War"), was written about AD 400 by Prudentius. The plot consists of the personified 'good' virtues of Hope, Sobriety, Chastity, Humility, etc. fighting the personified 'evil' vices of Pride, Wrath, Paganism, Avarice, etc. The personifications are women, because in Latin words for abstract concepts are in the feminine gender; an uninformed reader of the work might take the story literally as a tale of many angry women fighting one another, because as the first 'pure' allegory Prudentius provides no context or explanation of the allegory.

In this same period of the early 5th century three other authors of importance to the history of allegory emerged: Claudian, Macrobius and Martianus Capella. Little is known of these authors, even if they were truly Christian or not, but we do know they handed down the inclination to express learned material in allegorical form, mainly through personification, which later became a standard part of medieval schooling methods.

Claudian's first work *In Rufinum* was an attack against the ruthless Rufinus and would become a model for the 12th century *Anticlaudianus*, a well known allegory for how to be an upstanding man. As well his *Rape of Prosperpine* was a litany of mythological allegories, personifications, and cosmological allegories. Macrobius wrote *Commentary of the Dream of Scipio* providing the Middle Ages with the tradition of a favorite topic, the allegorical treatment of dreams.

Lastly Martianus wrote *Marriage of Philology and Mercury*, the title referring to the allegorical union of intelligent learning with the love of letters. It contained short treatises on the "seven liberal arts" (grammar, rhetoric, dialectic, geometry, arithmetic, astronomy, music) and thus became a standard textbook, greatly influencing educators and students throughout the Middle Ages.

Lastly, perhaps the most influential author of Late Antiquity was Boethius, in whose work *Consolation of Philosophy* we are first introduced to the personified Lady Philosophy, the source of innumerable later such personified figures.

2

Medieval Indian Literature

The cultural, political and historical map of Indian during the 11th century is vastly different from the contemporary 20th century, with India playing host to foreign invasions, military conquests, changes in weaponry and mode of warfare, changing conventions of socio-economic inert-relations and of course, the birth, growth and development of all the modern Indian languages and literatures written in them.

The Middle Ages in India were an incessant period of perpetual flux and fluctuation. Ordinary life during medieval period was far rosy from as is assumed now, and even more far from literature; on the contrary, life was exceedingly complex, undergoing fast changes. The continuous influx of migratory population brought with it different beliefs, customs, practices and life-styles, turning major portions of India into an ablaze pot.

The spread of philosophical movements or the sublime popularity of these genres, cultivated innate resources and responses to external forces were bettered to be prepared for the worse. The end result to this period a vibrant kaleidoscope of language and literature, that absolutely mirrored and reflected upon these themes of competition between two dominant religions: Hinduism and Islam. Medieval Indian literature wholly banked upon these themes, creating its own distinctive history in the long run.

Medieval period was also recognised by umpteen social movements, which out-and-out assayed to contest the prevailing orthodoxy and dogmatism, that was propagated by the so-called keepers of both Hindu and Muslim religions. These reformist movements accomplished heavy-weight mass support and were in totality clubbed under the idiom 'Bhakti Movement.'

The key players of the Bhakti Movement were Guru Nanak, the founder of Sikh religion, Kabir and numerous Sufi saints. They together echoed religious harmony and ostracised intolerance, Casteism and pomposity. These reformers, armed with their writings, verses or oral preachings, played a sizeable role in bridging the emotional chasm between practitioners of two predominant religions of India of that age. This aided in the essential pluralistic trait of India to re-emerge in the historical perspective, all of which were once again mirrored in the striking medieval Indian literatures.

Though orthodoxy ruled in medieval India and consequently trammeled the process of learning and hence scientific and academic pursuits to some extent, yet, medieval Indian literature bears its very first proof in authoritative biographies written. Baburnama by Mughal Emperor Babur himself, depicts Hindustan with grand prose, though with a rather distorted view. Ain-i-Akbari and Akbarnama by Abul Fazal are some of the only other instances of the vast body of biographies mothered during the Mughal era.

Furthermore, the verses of the Sufi saints and other saint poets of the Bhakti movement in medieval India, produced a literature for the first time, which was 'sensitive to the aspirations of the masses'. Numerous regional languages like Hindi, Urdu, Marathi, Bengali, etc., also achieved their distinguishing identities during the Mughal era, which in later eras, helped to generate a vast body of classic regional literature.

Tulsidas After a brief period of pre-literary authorships like inscriptions and official documents of a factual disposition, the new languages which entered into a stage of full-fledged development started translating, adapting and trans-creating literary works from ancient languages like Sanskrit. One of the features of early medieval Indian literature is several of these languages is the revitalisation which constitutes intrinsically a re-creation of the classics of ancient Indian literature.

Epics like Ramayana and Mahabharata received a rebirth in these newly formulated languages. Other ancient works like Panchatantra and numerous other Puranas and myths, came to be retold. Creating an inter-relation between these classics and modern languages, the authors like Kampan in Tamil, Krittivas Ojha in Bengali, Sarala Das in Oriya, Ezhuttacchan in Malayalam, Tulsi Das in Hindi and Nannaya in Telugu, stood out for the common mass.

As a substantial piece of information, this phase of medieval Indian literature provides a parallel to the literature of the Renaissance in Europe in the 15th-16th century, when the Graeco-Roman classics were retold and re-interpreted in a cotemporary expression.

Geography was yet another significant factor in the evolution of these medieval Indian literatures. The migratory nature of population in the early centuries were substituted by more or less settled living, and the reactions to the objects of nature, landscapes, seasons, flora and fauna have a lot to do with the conditioning of Indian literature during Middle Ages. The vocabulary and imagery of the writers were immensely influenced by the geographical location of the community to which the writer belonged, as is evidenced by the language and style of early Manipuri writers, as an example.

The rivers of India were greatly celebrated in medieval Indian literature, be it Brahmaputra, Ganga, Yamuna, Godavari, Kaveri or Sutlej. Apart from apparent and explicit references, there were subtle ways in which nature penetrated into literary works. The hills of Manipur, the rivers of Upper India, the desert of Rajasthan, the panorama of Konkan and Kerala, the snow-topped peaks of Kashmir - all of these have furnished staple poetic themes for medieval literature.

The regional grouping of literatures on the basis of ethnic similarity or geographical proximity or through mutual give-and-take is yet another feature established in medieval Indian literature. Both thematic and stylistic aspects had aided to form this proximity. Assamese, Bengali and Oriya manifest this; Assamese, Bengali and Maithili too, or even Gujarati, Hindi and Rajasthani. It is also noticed that at times the same writers made use of differentl languages. Tamil and Malayalam form another sub-group in this manner; Kannada and Telugu are the last to join this group. Even more unique in medieval Indian literature was the fact that these features were not merely superficial, they hint to deeper, underlying, complex aesthetic preferences and preconceptions. The multiple versions of the Heer-Ranjha story in Punjabi, of Sassi and Punnu in Sindhi, of Radha and Krishna in Oriya or Hindi or Sanskrit, of man and God in Sufi poetry in Kashmiri, Punjabi or Urdu, are materialisations of continuous give-and-take between groups of speakers of these languages.

Kabir Yet another significant feature in medieval Indian literature is the complete disappearance of women writers related to a work on a massive scale - long epics or full-scale drama. Yet the mystical thought of Lal Dyad, the devotional commitment of Mira Bai, the metaphysical reach of Avvayyar, the spirit of dedication of Akkamahadevi and the crystalline sadness of Habba Khatoon are among the high points of medieval Indian poetry.

Several of the medieval Indian literature and their earliest works in many of the various regional languages were sectarian, designed to advance or to celebrate particular unorthodox regional beliefs. Illustrations are the Caryapadas in Bengali, Tantric verses of the 12th century and the Lilacaritra (circa 1280), in Marathi. In Kannada (Kanarese) from the 10th century and later in Gujarati from the 13th century, the first strictly indigenous works comprise Jain romances. Ostensibly portraying the lives of Jain saints, these are actually popular tales based on Sanskrit and Pali themes.

Other examples in medieval Indian literature include in Rajasthani, relating about the bardic tales of chivalry and heroic resistance to the first Muslim invasions, such as the 12th century epic poem Prithirajaraso by Chand Bardai of Lahore. Most important of all, for later medieval Indian literature, were the first tinctures in the vernacular languages of the northern Indian cults of Krishna and Rama. Included in this phase are the 12th century poems by Jayadeva, named the Gitagovinda (The Cowherd's Song). and approximately 1400, a group of religious love poems written in Maithili (eastern Hindi of Bihar) by the poet Vidyapati were a decisive influence on the cult of Radha-Krishna in Bengal.

During the same period, the pathbreaking Bhakti Movement founded in South India was led by 63 nayanars (devotees of Shiva) and 12 Alvars (devotees of Vishnu). The most famous shaiva bhakta cults were the 4 Nalvar, namely—Snndarar, Appar, Sambandarand Manikkavasagar. Their devotional hymns, intrinsically linked with medieval Indian literature, are known to be doused in complete ecstasy and lyrics. The hymns of the 12 Alvars are held together as the Nalayira Divya Prabandham and chanted in temple rituals. Chief amongst them however is Andal, the only female Vaishnava saint and her hymns express the bridal mysticism in Hindu religion.

The path of devotion ushered by these mystics would later go on to influence Ramanuja and Madhavacharya philosophy. The Virashaiva Movement was incidental to spread the philosophy of Basavanna. Even the Haridasa Movement circularised from present day Karnataka had presented themselves in two groups—Vyasakuta (proficient in Vedas, Upanishads and Darshans) and Dasakuta (sect who conveyed the message of Madhavacharya through local Kannada language). Medieval Indian literature, however it had been influenced, was ultimately pivoted around this Bhakti Movement and its various unusual first-time revolutions by revolutionists. The

Bhakti movement also resulted in a proliferation of Kannada poetic works in praise of Vishnu. Eminent poets in this category comprise Purandara Dasa and Kanaka Dasa, whose contributions to Carnatic music were invaluable and still irreplaceable.

Chaitanya Mahaprabhu The spread of Bhakti Movement in North India was spontaneous and was centred around Lords Rama and Krishna. However, all forms of Bhakti Movement, both for the Muslims and Hindus, peacefully coexisted and were immeasurably popular with the masses.

The period within 14th-17th century A.D. witnessed the wave of Bhakti Movement sweeping across North India and teachers of this movement were saints like Vallabhacharya, Mira Bai, Kabir, Tulsidas, Tukaram and various other unknown entities, lost with the gradually accumulating sands of time. All of these personas were substantial to amplify the scope of medieval Indian literature, who penned in vernacular prose and poetry in the ethnic language of the state, employing simple language to express their devotional ecstasy and rapturous transformation.

Even seminal works in the regional languages on the theme of Bhakti are explored in Shyama Sangeet in Bengal, which were composed by Ram Prasad Sen and are still considered an integral part of Bengali culture. Dedicated to Goddess Kali, they medieval Indian literary outbursts are defined as allegorical mediums of spontaneous expressions.

It is alleged that Ram Prasad Sen use to held one-on-one dialogues with the Mother Goddess Kali through his poetry. Another Bengali leader in Bhakti movement was Chaitanya Mahaprabhu, who defined his system of philosophy as "achintya bheda bhed" (inconceivable and simultaneous oneness and difference). Chaitanya's philosophy presently is taught globally at the Hare Krishna movement.

As a final closing feature to medieval Indian literature, perhaps is the most contemporary and ahead of times aspect of love and war. Conflicts and tensions of all kinds dominated the atmosphere in umpteen medieval literatures in India. Love, not only the love of God or of fellowmen, but love in the domestic scenario, more precisely, the lover-and-beloved relationship. This was the staple theme in ghazals and mathnavis, in kirtans and padas, in tirhutis and abhangas. Some of the great romances from foreign sources as well as native sources came to be retold again and again in several languages. Apart from the old wars recounted in epics and puranas, war as an aspect of 'contemporary experience' also aroused the imagination of the medieval poet. The heroic sentiment is especially strong in Punjabi, Rajasthani, Tamil and Marathi literatures. In matters of love, the failure of love was as much a source of inspiration as the triumph of love. There exists an implicit glorification of the tragic in all the folk narratives on Heer-Ranjha or Sassi-Punnu or Yusuf-Zulaikha legends.

Bhakti Period in Literature

The Bhakti movement in India took place as an effort to inculcafe loving devotion and belief in God. The Bhakti movement in India aimed at the principle of monotheism, i.e. existence of one God. It started in the South of India and slowly spread to the north of India. This happened during the later half of the medieval period in the history of India (800-1700 A.D). The real essence of Bhakti is found in the great epics like Mahabharata and Ramayana. The Vedic scriptures also talk about the concept of pure devotion of God.

Many saints and devotional preachers led the Bhakti movement in different parts of the country. In south, around 63 Nayanars or Shaivite devotees organized and led the movement. They believed in the fact that true knowledge can be achieved only through selfless devotion and worship of the Supreme Power. The Bhakti movement of the Vaishnavaites and that of the Shaiva were simultaneous and started almost together. The Bhakti movements started then, have left an indelible mark in human beliefs and faiths.

The Bhakti movement started the trend of elaborate rituals in worship places. Devotional hymns in Temples, Qawalli in Mosques, Gurbani in Gurudwaras, etc. all came from the Bhakti movement. Chanting or taking the name of God was considered essential by many saints including the great Adi Shankaracharya. The significance of Bhakti movement was that it could be accessed by anyone, since all it needed was to remember God with full devotion and love.

The esteemed philosophical schools only changed the thoughts, but the Bhakti movement changed the entire perspective of a human. It went beyond artificial beliefs and rituals and encouraged people to have just complete faith in Almighty. The Bhakti movement in India gave a rich collection of literature based on devotion, spirituality, faith and numerous devotional hymns and chants

The medieval Hindi literature and its sufficient maturation was marked by the influence of Bhakti Movement and compilation of lengthy, epic poems.

Avadhi and Brij Bhasha were the primary dialects in which literature in Hindi was developed. The principal works in Avadhi include Malik Muhammad Jayasi's Padmavat and Tulsidas's Ṛamacharitamanas. The foremost works in Braj dialect are Tulsidas's Vinaya Patrika and Śurdas's Sur Sagar. Sadhukaddi was also a language used for wide reasons, especially by Kabir in his poetry and dohas.

The Bhakti kal or devotional period in Hindi literature also was accentuated by great theoretical development in poetry forms, predominantly from a blend of older forms of poetry in Sanskrit School and the Persian School. These included Verse Patterns like Doha (two-liners), Sortha, Chaupaya (four-liners), etc. This was also the epoch when Poetry was differentiated under the various Rasas. Distinct from the Adi Kaal (also stated as the VirGatha Kaal), which was characterised by an overindulgence into Poetry in the Vir Rasa (Heroic Poetry), the Bhakti kal had marked a much more sundry and vibrant form of poetry, which spanned the whole ambit of rasas, from Shringara rasa (Beauty), Vatsalya Rasa (Love), Vir Rasa (Heroism), Prema Rasa (Romance) etc.

Bhakti Kal or the Devotional Period in Hindi literature had extended within the time period of 14th and the 17th centuries. Coming basically under the medieval period in India, the country had by then been almost seized by Muslim rulers and their Islamic region. As such, the Bhakti kal had witnessed Islamic customs almost being upon thrust the common populace, and Hindus consequentially being quite demoralised at the outcome on their culture. Poets from the devotional period sensed that it was their moral duty to stimulate and stir a sense of devotion throughout religious poetry. These poets have since been classed into two groups, comprising: Nirguna and Saguna poets, depending upon their devotional attitude towards the Lord. Nirgunas have been further sub-divided into two classes, on the basis of the different sadhanas (disciplines) espoused by them.

Those that laid emphasis on the importance of knowledge for the realisation of the Omnipresent, were referred to as the 'Saint poets'. Kabir Das, Guru Nanak, Dharma Das, Maluk Das, Dadudayal, Sunder Das precisely belong to this genre in Hindi literature. The Saint poets through their Sakhis (couplets) and Padas (songs), had condemned rituals and had accentuated upon the theory of 'Monotheism'. Poets who conceived that love was the sole path to realise God, were referred to as Sufi Poets, a significant development in the advancing Hindi literature. Jayasi, Manjhan, Kutuban and Usman were the pioneers of this school of writing and belief. Poets belonging to the Saguna style are also classed into two groups, including: the followers of Rama and those of Krishna.

Tulsidas is the leading poet of the former group together with Agra Das, Nabha Das and Pran Chand Chauhan. Tulsidas portrays Rama as the Ideal Man in his classical works Ramacharitamanas, Gitavali, Kavitavali and Vinay Patrika.

The devotees of Krishna have, however, redrawn him according to his popular image, that of the playful Krishna. These poets like Surdas, Nand Das, Parmananda Das and Mirabai have voraciously penned about the Love and Beauty. The Devotional Period or Bhakti kal in Hindi literature indeed had given rise to 'immortal literature' and is distinguished as the Golden Age of Hindi Poetry.

Bhakti kal in Hindi literature was also the age of remarkable integration between the Hindu and Islamic elements in Arts. This integration had been possible primarily with the arrival of umpteen Muslim Bhakti poets like Abdul Rahim Khan-I-Khana, who was a court poet to Mughal emperor Akbar and was an ardent devotee of Krishṇa. The Nirgun School of Bhakti Poetry was also enormously secular in nature and its propounders like Kabir and Guru Nanak attracted a large number of followers, regardless of caste or religion.

Literature During Gupta Age

The Gupta kings encouraged literature. Not only in the arena of traditional Sanskrit literature but colossal development in other worldly literature in the form of poetry, drama and plays also made the Gupta empire to stand out in pride.

The Kavyas: Kalidasa was the greatest poet of the Gupta age. Generally majority of scholars have accepted the fact that Kalidasa was the contemporary of Chandragupta II, Vikramaditya. Among Kalidasa's poems the Ritusamhara is regarded as his earliest production. In this poem he has beautifully described the beauties of six seasons and their reaction on the human mind. The delicate observation of living sympathy with nature that are described here are truly Kalidasian in character. His Meghaduta is a pioneer duta kavya in Sanskrit literature. The stanzas in which Kalidasa describes the pining human heart of the youthful husband separated from his spouse are unrivalled for lofty imagery, unique metaphors and heroic hyperboles in Sanskrit literature. In the Kumarasarhbhava, which describes the union of Siva and Parvati in marriage and the birth of their son Kumara i.e. Kartikeya, Kalidasa exhibits richer variety and greater brilliance of fancy. The poet's power of description makes every scene appear to move before the reader's eyes. The Raghvarhsa is universally regarded as the finest specimen of Sanskrit mahakavyas as well.

The poetry of Kalidasa is characterized by grace, simplicity and also sentiment. They are always decorated by striking figures of speech. He is famous for his similes. In characterization he has few equals. He is superb in describing the emotions of love and pathos. His love of nature is as unique as his power of describing it. The works of Kalidasa are also valuable for the ideals, which they place before the society. By studying them the reader knows the Hindu ideals and also about the duties and responsibilities of persons in different classes of society and in various stages of life. His writings abound with pithy sayings containing salutary or good advice couched in beautiful language. From these writings persons in all walks of life can derive immense benefit.

Two other mahakavyas may be mentioned which are remarkable in that era. One is the Janakiharana written in the timeframe 517-526 A.D. by Kumaradasa and the other is the Kiratarjuniya by Bharavi written in c. 550 A.D. Both in manner and also in general treatment Kumaradasa imitates Kalidasa but is not able to reach the latter's height and grandeur. Bharavi's power of description and dignity of style impresses the reader but his literary gymnastics lessen the effect instead of enhancing the poetic impression.

Inscriptions: The Allahabad Pillar inscription of Samudragputa by his court poet Harisena and the

Mandasor inscription by Vatsabhatti possess some characteristics features of Sanskrit Kavya.. Three other inscriptions may be mentioned in this connection and these can be named as the Junagadh inscription, the Mehrauli iron pillars inscription and the Mandasor inscription of Yasovarman by Vasula. All the three inscriptions show considerable literary merit.

Dramas: Most probably bhasa flourished in the second or third century A.D. Thirteen plays are attributed to him. The plots of two of these have been derived from the Ramayana. They show little ingenuity on the part of the author. Six plays are based on the Mahabharata. They show the author in better relief. Four plays are based on current story literature. Of all the thirteen plays of Bhasa, the Svapnavasavadatta is the best. The plot construction of Bhasa is quite crude and certain incidents are repeated also. But Bhasa's style is simple and direct. It does not involve long compounds and too frequent embellishments. He sometime violates the rules of the Natyasastra.

Another predecessor of Kalidasa was Sudraka. He is the author of the famous drama, the Mrcchakatika. It is a unique work in Sanskrit dramatic literature. Sudraka most probably flourished in the earlier part of the fourth century A.D. Thus he may be considered the first Sanskrit dramatist of the Gupta period. Unlike the majority of Sanskrit dramatists the author has exhibited a surprising sense of fact, which completely dominates reason or imagination in this play. Action and characters in this play are portrayed directly from life. For variety of incidents and characters taken from different strata of society and the genuine humor, there is hardly anything in Sanskrit dramatic literature to compare with the Mrchchhakatika. The Mudraraksasa by Visakhadatta presents a true and surprisingly living picture of an ancient Indian court with all its political suspicions and intrigues. It is a great play in its own way. Kalidasa represents the high watermark of India's creative genius as in epic, lyrical poetry and also in drama. Of the three plays of Kalidasa the Malavikagnimitra is clearly an immature production. The Vikramorvasiya shows a great advance in Kalidasa's poetic and dramatic art.

In the portrayal of Pururavas, the poet has reached a lyrical height unknown to the conventional erotic plays in Sanskrit. In that poem ardent but hopeless distraction caused by Urvasi's disappearance and his mad search for this beloved has depicted in a unique manner. The theme of love reaches its highest consummation in Kalidasa's third play, the Abhijnanasakuntalam.

In this play Kalidasa treats love as a factor in the scheme of larger life and not merely as an isolated individual passion. In this play Kalidasa also shows his great dramatic genius in the regular development of the plot. He has worked a lot in the proportions of the cast, the happy choice of incidents, the majesty and charm of the stage effects, etc. His rich imagery and fine appreciation of nature, his grace and above all, his noble rhythm has taken the poem in its height.

In Kalidasa's dramas, imagination dominates over sense of fact and reason, while in the Mrchchakatika sense of fact dominates over reason and imagination. With the solitary exception of the Mrchchhakatika, the dramas of the Gupta period are actually the dramas of kings and court life.

The peculiar conditions and environments of the Gupta age had some effect on the literature produced during the period. Under the influence of the royal courts, Sanskrit poetry tended to become more and more aristocratic in character. It attempted to cater to the tastes of the higher and refined classes of the society and thus remained to the extent isolated from the life of the common people as well. Also the ethical and didactic literature made its presence felt during this Gupta period.

The Panchatantra is a storybook of that era. It seems to have been originally composed with a view to imparting to young princes instruction in political science and practical conduct. Visnu Sarma is the author of this book. The earlier version of the Panchatantra was known as the Tantrakhyayika, which was most probably, composed in the timeframe of C. 250 A.D. The Panchatantra version was written some time during the Gupta period.

The book was so popular that about 200 versions of the book exist in more than 50 languages of the world. It was translated into Pahalavi before 570 A.D. and soon after it was translated into the Syrian and the Arabic languages. It reached Europe before the 11th century A.D. Its versions into Greek, Latin, Spanish, Italian, German, English and old Slavonic languages had come into existence before the close of the 16th century A.D.

Bhartrhari in the era of C. 600-650 A.D. composed the Srngarasataka. The first sataka contains general observations on love and women, the second sataka deals with life of virtue and wisdom and the third sataka deals with life of renunciation. Probably these three satakas were composed towards the end of the Gupta period.

Grammar: On account of the works of Panini, Katyayana and Patanjali on Sanskrit grammar there was hardly any scope for composing a book on Sanskrit grammar. The earliest work of the Gupta period on this Sanskrit grammar is most probably the Katantra of Sarvavarman. It is simple Sanskrit grammar. Buddhist scholar of Bengal, Chandragomin composed the Chandravyakarana, which was very popular in Kashmir, Nepal and Tibet and later reached Sri Lanka. Probably he lived in the last decades of the sixth century A.D. He has made some original contribution to Sariskrit grammar as well.

Bhartrhari composed the Vakyapadiya, which deals with philosophy of language in general, and discusses sentence and word in Sanskrit language.

Lexicography: The most famous lexicographical work in Sanskrit is the Namalinganusasana of Amarasirhha, better known as Amara-kosa. It is the oldest work on lexicography. Amarasirhha was a Buddhist, yet his book has become most popular even among the Hindus.

Prosody: The Srutabodha is a handbook on metres. Varahamihira also deals with metres in the Brhatsamhita. There is also a section in the Agni Purana, which deals with the same.

Painting: A section of the Visnudharmottara Purana deals with painting and gives detailed instructions about surface preparation in fresco paintings and the use of different colors in them.

Literature During Harsha's Reign

In the field of literature and education many significant changes had taken place during Harsha's reign. In the field of literature and education many significant changes had taken place during Harsha's reign. Education had made a remarkable progress during this period. Educational centers were also opened along with the Buddhist monasteries and other religious centers. Most of these centers were situated in Kannauj, Monghyr, Manikpur, Gaya etc. Nalanda University had reached the zenith of its glory and significance in Harsha's period. Besides, religion, other subjects such as philosophy, medical science etc. were also taught. The educational system was to a great extent has on arguments and debates. The standards of the students of Nalanda were very high.

The number of student coming from foreign countries to study at Nalanda included considerably larger number of Chinese students. About hundred Chinese travelers came to receive education at Nalanda.

Besides Nalanda, Ujjain was another important centre of education where especially astrology and mathematics were taught. Taxila was also an important centre of education. Besides these universities, education was imparted in many other centers.

King Harsha was himself a great poet and dramatist; the three dramas 'Priyadarshika,' 'Ratnavali' are attributed to him.

The famous literary works, 'Harshacharit' and 'Kadambari' were written by Bana during Harsha's period. Great power Bharavi and the famous scholar Shilabhadra were also there during his reign. Achraya jayasena was also in the court of Harsha.

Thus there had been a great progress in the field of literature and education during Harsha's period, and it is due to this that this period occupies an important position in the history of India. It is on account of this feature that this age has been praised by different scholars. Hiuen Tsang was astonished and very much impressed to see the progress of education and literature in those days.

Eminent Medieval Authors

Mirabai

Mirabai was a great saint and devotee of Sri Krishna. Despite facing criticism and hostility from her own family, she lived an exemplary saintly life and composed many devotional bhajans. Historical information about the life of Mirabai is a matter of some scholarly debate. The oldest biographical account was Priyadas's commentary in Nabhadas' Sri Bhaktammal in 1712. Nevertheless there are many aural histories, which give an insight into this unique poet and Saint of India.

Early Life

Mira was born around the start of the 16th Century in the Chaukari village in Merta, Rajasthan. Her father was Ratan Singh a descendent of Rao Rathor, the founder of Jodhpur. When Mirabai was only 3 years old, a wandering Sadhu came to her family's home and gave a doll of Sri Krishna to her father. Her father took this is as a special blessing, but was initially unwilling to give it to her daughter, because she felt she would not appreciate it. However Mira had, at first sight, become deeply enamoured with this doll. She refused to eat until the doll of Sri Krishna was given to her. To Mira, this figure of Sri Krishna, embodied his living presence. She resolved to make Krishna her lifelong friend, lover, and husband. Throughout her turbulent life she never wavered from her youthful commitment.

On one occasion when Mira was still young she saw a wedding procession going down the street. Turning to her mother she asked in innocence, "Who will be my husband?" Her mother replied, half in jest, half in seriousness. "You already have your husband, Sri Krishna." Mira's mother was supportive of her daughter's blossoming religious tendencies, but she passed away when she was only young.

At an early age Mira's father arranged for her to be married to Prince Bhoj Raj, who was the eldest son of Rana Sanga of Chittor. They were an influential Hindu family and the marriage significantly elevated Mira's social position. However Mira was not enamoured of the luxuries of the palace. She served her husband dutifully, but in the evening she would spend her time in devotion and singing to her beloved Sri Krishna. Whilst singing devotional bhajans, she would frequently lose awareness of the world, entering into states of ecstasy and trance.

Go to that impenetrable realm
That death himself trembles to look upon.
There plays the fountain of love
With swans sporting on its waters.

Conflict with Family

However her new family did not approve of her piety and devotion to Krishna. To make things worse Mira refused to worship their family deity Durga. She said she had already committed herself to Sri Krishna. Her family became increasingly disproving of her actions, but the fame and saintly reputation of Mirabai spread throughout the region. Often she would spend time discussing spiritual issues with Sadhus and people would join in the singing of her bhajans. However this just made her family even more jealous. Mira's sister-in-law Udabai started to spread false gossip and defamatory remarks about Mirabai. She said Mira was entertaining men in her room. Her husband, believing these stories to be true, tore into her room with sword in hand. However he saw Mira only playing with a doll. No man was there at all. Yet throughout these hysterical slanders Mirabai remained unmoved by both the criticism and praise of the world.

> This infamy, O my Prince
> is delicious!
> Some revile me,
> others applaud,
> I simply follow my incomprehensible road
> A razor thin path
> but you meet some good people,
> A terrible path but you hear a true word
> Turn back?
> Because the wretched stare and see nothing?
> O Mira's Lord is noble and dark,
> and slanderers
> rake only themselves
> over the coals

Mirabai and Akbar

Mira's fame spread far and wide her devotional bhajans were sung across northern India. It is said that the fame and spirituality of Mirabai reached the ears of the Moghul Emperor Akbar. Akbar was tremendously powerful, but he was also very interested in different religious paths. The problem was that he and Mirabai's family were the worst enemies; to visit Mirabai would cause problems for both him and Mirabai. But Akbar was determined to see Mirabai, the Princess – Saint. Disguised in the clothes of beggars he travelled with Tansen to visit Mirabai. Akbar was so enamoured of her soulful music and devotional singing, that he placed at her feet a priceless necklace before leaving. However in the course of time Akbar's visit came to the ears of her husband Bhoj Raj. He was furious that a Muslim and his own arch enemy and set eyes upon his wife. He ordered Mirabai to commit suicide by drowning in a river. Mirabai intended to honour her husbands command, but as she was entering the river Sri Krishna appeared to her and commanded her to leave for Brindaban where she could worship him in peace. So with a few followers, Mirabai left for Brindaban, where she spent her time in devotion to Sri Krishna. After a while her husband became repentant, feeling that her wife was actually a real saint. Thus he travelled to Brindaban and requested her to return. Mirabai agreed, much to the displeasure of the rest of her family.However soon after Mira's husband died (fighting in battles with the Moghul emperors). This made the situation even worse for Mirabai. Her father in law, Rana Sanga, saw her husband's death as a way to be rid of Mirabai. He commanded her to commit Sati. However Mirabai, with the inner direct assurance of her beloved Sri Krishna, said that she would not do this. Her real husband, Sri Krishna had not died. She would later say in her poetry.

> *"sati na hosyan girdhar gansyan mhara man moho ghananami",*
>
> "I will not commit sati. I will sing the songs of Girdhar Krishna, and will not become sati because my heart is enamoured of Hari."

After this experience her family continued to torture her. They restricted her movements and sought to make her life as uncomfortable as possible. Yet in the face of all these trials and tribulation she remained detached from her physical suffering. There was nothing that could disturb her inner connection to Giridhara (epithet of Sri Krishna as young cowherd boy). It is said that twice her family tried to kill her, once through a venomous snake and once through poisonous drink. On both occasions it is said Mirabai, protected by the Grace of Sri Krishna, came to no ill harm.

Mirabai in Brindaban

However the relentless torments and hostility interfered with her life of devotion and contemplation on Krishna. She sought the advice of learned men and Saints. They advised her to leave the palace and return to Brindaban. Secretly with some followers she slipped out of the palace and escaped to the holy city of Brindaban. In Brindaban Mirabai was free to worship Giridhara to her heart's content. She would spend her time in singing bhajans and in ecstatic communion with Krishna. Like a true Bhakti she worshipped God wholeheartedly. The riches of the world offered no attraction to Mirabai; her only satisfaction came from her single minded devotion to Sri Krishna. Her soul was ever yearning for Krishna. She considered herself to be a Gopi of Vrindaban, mad only with pure love for Krishna.

> I am mad with love
> And no one understands my plight.
> Only the wounded
> Understand the agonies of the wounded,
> When the fire rages in the heart.

Only the jeweller knows the value of the jewel,
Not the one who lets it go.
In pain I wander from door to door,
But could not find a doctor.
Says Mira: Harken, my Master,
Mira's pain will subside
When Shyam comes as the doctor.

Her devotion and spiritual magnetism were infectious. She inspired many to follow the path of Vaishnavism. As Swami Sivananda stated:

> "Mira wafted the fragrance of devotion far and wide. Those who came in contact with her were affected by her strong current of Prem. Mira was like Lord Gauranga. She was an embodiment of love and innocence. Her heart was the temple of devotion. Her face was the lotus-flower of Prem. There was kindness in her look, love in her talk, joy in her discourses, power in her speech and fervour in her songs."

Even learned Sadhus would come to her for inspiration. There is a story of one respected Spiritual Master, who refused to speak to Mirabai because she was a woman. Mirabai replied there was only 1 real man in Brindaban, Sri Krishna; everyone else was a Gopi of Krishna. On hearing this the Spiritual teacher accepted the wisdom of Mirabai and agreed to talk to her. Later Mirabai would become his student.

Poems of Mirabai

Much of what we know about Mirabai comes from her poetry. Her poetry express the longing and seeking of her soul for union with Sri Krishna. At time she expresses the pain of separation and at other times the ecstasy of divine union. Her devotional poems were designed to be sung as bhajans and many are still sung today.

> "Mira's songs infuse faith, courage, devotion and love of God in the minds of the readers. They inspire the aspirants to take to the path of devotion and they produce in them a marvellous thrill and a melting of the heart."

Mirabai was a devotee of the highest order. She was immune to the criticism and suffering of the world. She was born a princess but forsook the pleasures of a palace for begging on the streets of Brindaban. She lived during a time of war and spiritual decline, but her life offered a shining example of the purest devotion. Many were inspired by her infectious devotion and spontaneous love for Sri Krishna. Mirabai showed how a seeker could attain union with God, only through love. Her only message was that Krishna was her all.

> My Beloved dwells in my heart,
> I have actually seen that Abode of Joy.
> Mira's Lord is Hari, the Indestructible.
> My Lord, I have taken refuge with Thee,
> Thy slave.

It is said in her death she melted into the heart of Krishna. Tradition relates how one day she was singing in a temple, when Sri Krishna appeared in his subtle form. Sri Krishna was so pleased with his dearest devotee. He opened up his heart centre and Mirabai entered leaving her body whilst in the highest state of Krishna consciousness.

Tukaram

Tukaram was born in 1608, in the small village of Dehu in the West Indian state of Maharashtra to Bolhoba and Kanakai a couple belonging to the lower Sudra class. He had two other brothers. Despite their lower class status the family was well to do and enjoyed good social standing in the village. Tukaram's troubles started with the illness of his father, due to which he had to start supporting his family at the tender age of thirteen. Shortly thereafter, both his parents died. Tukaram's problems only mounted; death of his family members and economic hardship seemed to plague him.

Tukaram was married twice, his first wife Rakhumabai died due to starvation during a famine, his second wife Jijabai or Avali as she was called, was much younger than his first had been and had little patience with his devotion and for God and she nagged him continuously. He had three sons. Tukaram was initiated without any intermediaries as the other saints usually were. He dreamt that he was initiated by the Lord Hari himself dressed as a Brahman.

Tukaram continuously sang the praises of the Lord, he sang it in the form of abhangs which he wrote. These were in his mother tongue Marathi. The abhangs express his feelings and philosophical outlook. During his 41 years, Tukaram composed over 5,000 abhangs. Many of them speak of events in his life, which make them somewhat autobiographical. Yet, they are focused on God, Pandurang, and not Tukaram. His abhangs became very popular with the masses of common people. It was this very popularity that caused the religious establishment (the high caste Brahmins) to hate and persecute Tukaram. as, he was causing them to lose their power over the people. There are many miracles attributed to Tukaram.

Vallabhacharya

Vallabhacharya was a Tailang Brahmana. He preached the worship of Vishnu in the form of Krishna. He was born in 1479 in the Telugu country. He visited Mathura, Vrindaban and many other sacred places and finally settled at Benaras.

VallabhacharyaVallabhacharya called his system of bhakti, Shuddhavaita. According to him, its God's grace alone that can lead one to Heaven. When Shri Vallabhacharya was on visit to northwest India, the Lord requested him to come to Mount Govardhan to meet Him. At this time the Lord revealed Himself to Shri Vallabh in form of Shree Nathji. At this time, the Lord hugged Shri Vallabhacharya and gave him sacred mantra "Shree Krishna: Sharnam Mama" to initiate people.

Pushtimarg, the path of divine grace is based on the "Vishudhadvaita" philosophy, initially shown by Shri Vallabhacharya. Shri Vallabh strongly suggested that Lord Shree Krishna is the ultimate God. Thus, Shri Krishna's blessings alone and only can free humans from the painful cycle of birth and death. Shri Vallabhacharya wrote many books, but many of them are not available today due to lack of proper perseverance. Many important books / articles / padas written by Vallabhacharya and the Acharyas of Vallabhkul are still available and famous in vaishnava society. Yamunashatakam, Navaratnam and many other padas, and Subodhinji book are very important for Vaishnavas to read and understand.

Vallabhacharya taught that there was no distinction between Brahmin and the individual soul and the latter could get rid of bondage by Bhakti. He asked his followers to offer everything in the service of Krishna. According to Vallabha only individuals who have the grace of Krishna can be successful in the path of devotion. He advocated the worship of idols of

Krishna. Later the rituals of this sect became very complicated. Many followers of Vallabha composed poems on Krishna in Hindi and thus contributed greatly to the spread of Krishna cult.

Shree Vallabhacharya was of modern thinking and that is why he started Mogul style attire for Shree Nathji. By following Vallabhacharya's method is an easy path towards the religious journey and since this is proven method why not adopt it as a gift rather than introducing new method which may be not suitable to the luxury of Purushottam.

Tulsidas

Tulsidas was a great Awadhi bhakta (devotee), philosopher, composer, and the author of *Ramacharitamanasa,* an epic poem and scripture devoted to the Hindu god Rama.

Ramacharitamanasa, an epic devoted to Rama, was the Awadhi version of Ramayana of Valmiki.It is not exactly the "Awadhi version", but the original one of its kind. Apart from "Awadhi"- three other languages are also seen in the epic Ramacharitamanasa- they are "Bhojpuri", " Brijbhasa" and "the local language of people of Chitrakut".Like many translations of the original Sanskrit Ramayana, it is read and worshipped with great reverence in many Hindu homes in India. It is an inspiring book that contains couplets in verse form called *chaupai.*

It is also called *Tulsi-krita Ramayana* and is as well known among Hindi-speaking Hindus in India. Many of its verses are popular proverbs in that region. Tulsidas' phrases have passed into common speech, and are used by millions of Hindi speakers (and even speakers of Urdu) without the speakers being conscious of their origin. Not only are his sayings proverbial: his doctrine actually forms the most powerful religious influence in present-day Hinduism; and, though he founded no school and was never known as a guru or master, he is everywhere accepted as both poet and saint, an inspired and authoritative guide in religion and the conduct of life.

Tulsidas professed himself the humble follower of his teacher, Narhari Das, from whom as a boy in Sukar-khet he first heard the tale of Rama's exploits that would form the subject of the *Ramacaritamanasa.* Narhari Das was the sixth in spiritual descent from Ramananda, a founder of popular Vaishnavism in northern India, who was also known for his famous poems.

There are numerous differences between Tulsi Ramacaritamanasa and Valmiki Ramayana. One example is the scene in which Kaikayi forces her husband to exile Rama. In Tulsi Das it becomes considerably longer and more psychological, with intense characterisation and brilliant similes.

Besides the *Ramacaritamanasa,* Tulsidas the author of five longer and six shorter works, most of them dealing with the theme of Rama, his doings, and devotion to him. The former are

— the *Dohavali,* consisting of, 573 miscellaneous doha and sortha verses; of this there is a duplicate in the Ram-satsai, an arrangement of seven centuries of verses, the great majority of which occur also in the Dohavali and in other works of Tulsi,

— the *Kabitta Ramayan* or *Kavitavali,* which is a history of Rama in the kavitta, ghanakshari, chaupaï and savaiya metres; like the

Ramacaritamanasa, it is divided into seven kandas or cantos, and is devoted to setting forth the majestic side of Rama's character,

- the *Gitavali,* also in seven kandas, aiming at the illustration of the tender aspect of the Lord's life; the metres are adapted for singing
- the *Krishnavali* or *Krishna gitavali,* a collection of 61 songs in honor of Krishna, in the Kanauji dialect of Hindi: the authenticity of this is doubtful,
- the *Vinaya Patrika,* or *Book of petitions,* a series of hymns and prayers of which the first 43 are addressed to the lower gods, forming Rama's court and attendants, and the remainder, Nos. 44 to 279, to Rama himself.

His minor works include Baravai Ramayana, Janaki Mangal, Ramalala Nahachhu, Ramajna Prashna, Parvati Mangal, Krishna Gitavali, Hanuman Bahuka, Sankata Mochana and Vairagya Sandipini. Of the smaller compositions the most interesting is the *Vairagya Sandipani,* or *Kindling of continence,* a poem describing the nature and greatness of a holy man, and the true peace to which he attains.

Tulsidas's most famous and read piece of literature apart from the Ramayana is the "Hanuman Chalisa", a poem praising Hanuman. Many Hindus recite it daily as a prayer. The entire collection of compositions by Tulsi Das, consisting of 13 books, has been translated into English by Binda Prasad Khattri (1898-1985). The work is however, yet unpublished.

Doctrine

Like Ramanuja, Tulsi believes in a supreme personal God, possessing all gracious qualities (sadguna), as well as in the quality-less (nirguna) neuter impersonal Brahman of Sankaracharya; this Lord Himself once took the human form, and became incarnate, for the blessing of mankind, as Rama. The body is therefore to be honored, not despised. The Lord is to be approached by faith (bhakti) disinterested devotion and surrender of self in perfect love, and all actions are to be purified of self-interest in contemplation of Him. Show love to all creatures, and thou wilt be happy; for when thou lovest all things, thou lovest the Lord, for He is all in all.

The soul is from the Lord, and is submitted in this life to the bondage of works (karma); Mankind, in their obstinacy, keep binding themselves in the net of actions, and though they know and hear of the bliss of those who have faith in the Lord, they don't attempt the only means of release. The bliss to which the soul attains, by the extinction of desire, in the supreme home, is not absorption in the Lord, but union with Him in abiding individuality. This is emancipation (mukti) from the burden of birth and rebirth, and the highest happiness.

Tulsi, as a Saryupareen Brahmin, venerates the whole Hindu pantheon, and is especially careful to give Shiva or Mahadeva, the special deity of the Brahmins, his due, and to point out that there is no inconsistency between devotion to Rama and attachment to Shiva. But the practical end of all his writings is to inculcate bhakti addressed to Rama as the great means of salvation and emancipation from the chain of births and deaths, a salvation which is as free and open to men of the lowest caste as to Brahmins.

The literary worth of Tulsidas has been highlighted by Acharya Ram Chandra Shukla in his critical work Hindi Sahitya Ka Itihaas.Acharya Shukla has elaborated Tulsi's Lokmangal as the doctrine for social upliftment which made this great poet immortal and comparable to any other world littérateur.

Sant Kabir

Sant Kabir is considered to be one of the greatest poets as well as mystics ever born in India. He believed that human beings are equal and being one with God is the ultimate aim of every individual. His love and devotion towards the Supreme One clearly reflects in his poetry. The Holy Guru Granth Sahib contains over 500 verses by the great saint, Kabir. The verses or dohas of Guru Kabir are still read by people with awe and admiration.

The story is told that on one particular day of the year, anyone can become a disciple by having a master speak the name of God over him. It is common for those who live near the Ganges to take their morning bath there in the sacred waters. The bhakti saint Ramananda took his bath as he did every day, by arising before dawn. On this special day, Ramananda awoke before dawn and found his customary way down to the steps of the Ganges.

As he was walking down the steps to the waters, a little hand reached out in the predawn morning and grabbed the saint's big toe. Ramananda was taken by surprise and he expressed his shock by calling out the name of God. Looking down he saw in the early morning light the hand of the young Kabir. After his bath in the early light he noticed that on the back of the little one's hand was written in Arabic the name

Kabir. He adopted him as son and disciple and brought him back to his ashrama, much to the disturbance of his Hindu students, some of whom left in righteous protest.

It is said that what really made this meeting special is that it was only after Kabir's enlightenment that Ramananda, his teacher, became enlightened.

Not much is known about what sort of spiritual training Kabir may have received. He did not become a sadhu nor did he ever abandon worldly life. Kabir chose instead to live the balanced life of a householder and mystic, a tradesman and contemplative.

Philosophies

Kabir was influenced by the prevailing religious mood of his times, such as old Brahmanic Hinduism, Hindu and Buddhist Tantrism, the teachings of Nath yogis and the personal devotionalism of South India mixed with the imageless God of Islam.The influence of these various doctrines is clearly evident in Kabir's verses. Eminent historians like R.C. Majumdar, P.N. Chopra, B.N. Puri and M.N. Das have held that Kabir is the first Indian saint to have harmonised Hinduism and Islam by preaching a universal path which both Hindus and Muslims could tread together. But there are a few critics who contest such claims.

The basic religious principles he espoused are simple. According to Kabir, all life is an interplay of two spiritual principles. One is the personal soul (*Jivatma*) and the other is God (*Paramatma*). It is Kabir's view that salvation is the process of bringing into union these two divine principles. Despite legend which claims Kabir met with Guru Nanak, their lifespans did not overlap. The incorporation of much of his verse in Sikh scripture, and the fact that Kabir was a predecessor of Nanak, have led some western scholars to mistakenly describe him as a forerunner of Sikhism.

His greatest work is the *Bijak* (the "Seedling"), an idea of the fundamental one. This collection of poems demonstrates Kabir's own universal view of spirituality. His vocabulary is replete with ideas regarding Brahman and Hindu ideas of karma and reincarnation. His Hindi was a vernacular, straightforward kind, much like his philosophies. He often advocated leaving aside the Qur'an and Vedas and simply following Sahaja path, or the Simple/ Natural Way to oneness in God. He believed in the Vedantic concept of *atman,* but unlike earlier orthodox Vedantins, he followed this philosophy to its logical end by spurning the Hindu societal caste system and worship of murti, showing clear belief in both *bhakti* and Sufi ideas. The major part of Kabir's work as a *bhagat* was collected by the fifth Sikh guru, Guru Arjan Dev, and forms a part of the Sikh scripture Guru Granth Sahib.

While many ideas reign as to who his living influences were, the only Guru of whom he ever spoke was *Satguru.* Hence one does not find any mention of human gurus in his verses.

Poetry Career

His poems resonate with praise for the true guru who reveals the divine through direct experience, and denounce more usual ways of attempting god-union such as chanting, austerities, etc. His verses, which being illiterate he never expressed in writing and were spoken in vernacular Hindi, often began with some strongly worded insult to get the attention of passers-by. Kabir has enjoyed a revival of popularity over the past half century as arguably the most accessible and understandable of the Indian saints, with a special influence over spiritual traditions such as those of Sant Mat, Garib Das and Radha Soami.

3

Medieval French Literature

Medieval French is written in Oïl languages (particularly Old French and early Middle French) during the period from the eleventh century to the end of the fifteenth century.

The material and cultural conditions in France and associated territories around the year 1100 unleashed what the scholar Charles Homer Haskins termed the "Renaissance of the 12th century" and, for over the next hundred years, writers, "jongleurs", "clercs" and poets produced an enormous quantity of remarkable creative works in all genres. Although the dynastic struggles of the Hundred Years' War and the international Black Death epidemic of the fourteenth century in many ways curtailed this creative production, the fifteenth century laid the groundwork for the French Renaissance.

Language

Up to roughly 1340, the Romance languages spoken in the Middle Ages in the northern half of what is today's France are collectively known as "ancien francais" ("Old French") or "langues d'oïl" (languages where one says "oïl" to mean "yes"): following the Germanic invasions of France in the fifth century, these Northern dialects had developed distinctly different phonetic and syntactical structures from the languages spoken in southern France (collectively known as "langues d'oc" or the Occitan language family, of which the largest group is the Provencal language). The Western peninsula of Brittany spoke Breton, a Celtic language. Catalan was spoken in the South, and Germanic languages and Franco-Provencal were spoken in the East.

The various dialects of Old French developed into what are recognised as regional languages today. Languages which developed from dialects of Old French include: Bourguignon, Champenois, Franc-Comtois, Francien (theoretical), Gallo, Lorrain, Norman, Anglo-Norman (spoken in England after the Norman Conquest of 1066), Picard, Poitevin, Saintongeais and Walloon.

Because of the Norman Conquest of England in 1066, medieval French literature also includes works produced in the Anglo-Norman realm, including England, from (1066-1204).

From 1340 to the beginning of the seventeenth century, a generalised French language became clearly distinguished from the other competing Oïl languages. This is referred to as Middle French ("moyen français").

The vast majority of literary production in Old French is in verse; the development of prose as a literary form was a late phenomenon (in the late Middle Ages, many of the romances and epics were converted into prose versions). The French language does not have a significant stress accent (like English) or long and short syllables (like Latin). This means that the French metric line is not determined by the number of beats, but by the number of syllables. The most common metric lengths are the ten-syllable line (decasyllable), the eight-syllable line (octosyllable) and the twelve-syllable line (the "alexandrine"). Verses could be combined in a variety of ways: blocks (of varying lengths) of assonanced (occasionally rhymed) lines are called "laisses"; another frequent form is the rhymed couplet. The choice of verse form was generally dictated by the genre. The Old French epics ("chansons de geste") are generally written in *ten-syllable assonanced "laisses"*, while the chivalric romance ("roman") was usually written in *octosyllabic rhymed couplets*.

Orality and Transmission

The Middle Ages was an oral culture; literacy was reserved for an educated elite of *clercs* and chancellery officials. Furthermore, before the advent of the printing press, all transcriptions were done by hand. These facts have a number of important implications for the history of French literature:

1. The very existence of a text implies that someone transcribed or wrote it. Mistakes in the transcription, or clerical censorship can affect the text that has survived. Different performances of the work produce different versions. Given the system of hand-written copies, errors and missed passages are common. In analysing medieval documents, scholars try to reconstruct—from all available copies of a text—the presumed state of the original performance or text, but this is often impossible. Certain stories—like *Tristan and Yseult* — exist only in a fragmentary state and were

probably never told as one complete narrative until the 13th century.

2. It is hard to judge in what way the work was originally performed. Was it read aloud, sung a cappella or accompanied with music? Did the "jongleur" use a script or improvise? This question of the possible "non-written composition" of highly organised literary works is directly linked to the "oral poet" controversy surrounding Homer.

The "book" in the Renaissance is usually called a codex; its pages are made from parchment or vellum (stretched lamb or calf skin) and these pages can be scraped and reused if needed. Experts have been able to use modern imaging techniques to rediscover some texts which have been abraded in this way. Medieval texts sometimes have illustrations; this is especially true of prestigious and devotional books for nobles. This form of illustration is called illumination. Illuminated manuscripts often have fanciful images that come from the medieval fable or from popular fiction. Much medieval poetry has come down to us in the form of chansonniers, which often include some form of musical notation.

A great number of medieval texts no longer exist; like many Latin and Greek works from the ancient world, fires, worms, floods, the reuse of books and disregard have eliminated many works that only exist today as titles in other works.

Early Texts

The earliest extant French literary texts date from the eleventh century. The first literary works written in Old French were saints' lives. The *Canticle of Saint*

Eulalie, written in the second half of the ninth century, is generally accepted as the first such text. It is a short poem that recounts the martyrdom of a young girl.

The best known of the early Old French saints' lives is the *Vie de Saint Alexis,* the life of Saint Alexis, a translation/rewriting of a Latin legend. Saint Alexis fled from his family's home in Rome on his wedding night and dwelled as a hermit in Syria until a mystical voice began telling people of his holiness. In order to avoid the earthly honor that came with such fame, he left Syria and was driven back to Rome, where he lived as a beggar at his family's house, unrecognised by all until his death.

Alexis was only identified later when the pope read his name in a letter held in the dead saint's hand. Although the saint left his family in order to devote his life more fully to God, the poem makes clear that his father, mother, and wife are saved by the Alexis' intercession and join him in Paradise. The earliest and best surviving text is in St. Albans Psalter, written probably at St Albans, England, in the second or third decade of the twelfth century.

The Chanson de Geste

At the beginning of the 13th century, Jean Bodel, in his *Chanson de Saisnes,* divided medieval French narrative literature into three subject areas:

1) The Matter of France or Matter of Charlemagne
2) The Matter of Rome—romances in an ancient setting
3) The Matter of Britain—Arthurian romances, Breton lais

The first of these is the subject area of the *chansons de geste* ("songs of exploits" or "songs of (heroic) deeds"), epic poems typically composed in ten-syllable assonanced (occasionally rhymed) *laisses*. More than one hundred *chanson de geste* have survived in around three hundred manuscripts. The chief theme of the earliest French epics was the court of Charlemagne, Charles Martel and Charles the Bald and their wars against the Moors and Saracens, or disputes between kings and their rebellious vassals.

The oldest and most celebrated of the *chansons de geste* is *The Song of Roland* (earliest version composed c. 1098), seen by some as the national epic of France (comparable with *Beowulf* in England, the *Song of the Nibelungs* in Germany and the *Song of Mío Cid* in Spain). It is perhaps no coincidence that the *Song of Roland* was first written down at a date very close to that of Pope Urban's call (1095) for the First Crusade; its plot may be seen as a glorification of the crusader ethos.

The earliest *chansons de geste* are (more or less) anonymous. They are popular literature (aimed at a warrior class, some say, though the evidence for this is inconclusive). They use an assortment of stock characters: the valiant hero, the brave traitor, the shifty or cowardly traitor, the Saracen, the giant, and so forth. But they also reveal much of the fears and conflicts that were part of the audience's experience. Kings are vain, foolish, old or wily. Insults that threaten honour or cause shame are seen to provoke bloody conflict, which may arise simply from competitiveness among knights or noble families. For discussion of the much debated origins of this epic genre.

Approximately one hundred *chansons* survive, in manuscripts that date from the twelfth to the fifteenth century. Not long after Jean Bodel (above), Bertrand de Bar-sur-Aube in his *Girart de Vienne* set out a grouping of the *chansons de geste* into three cycles, each named after a chief character or ancestral figure, and each with a central theme, such as loyalty to a feudal chief, or the defence of Christianity. This is a list of the cycles with a few of the *chansons* that belong to each:

1) The Geste du roi: In these the chief character was Charlemagne or his heirs, and a pervasive theme was his role as the divine champion of Christianity. This cycle contains the earliest and best known of the epics:
   a) *The Song of Roland* (1098 for the Oxford text, the earliest version: several others exist, including an Occitan version)
   b) *Fierabras* (1170)
   c) *Aspremont* (1190-1200)
   d) *Huon de Bordeaux* (1216-1268)
   e) *Chanson de Saisnes* by Jean Bodel (1200)
2) The Geste de Garin de Monglane, whose central character was William of Orange. These dealt with knights who were typically younger sons without an inheritance who sought land and glory through combat with the Saracens.
   a) *Chanson de Guillaume* (1100)
   b) *Couronnement de Louis* (1130)
   c) *Charroi de Nîmes* (1140)
   d) *Prise d'Orange* (1150)
   e) *Aliscans* (1165)

f) *Aymeri de Narbonne* and *Girart de Vienne* by Bertrand de Bar-sur-Aube (1190-1217)

3) The Geste de Doon de Mayence (or the "rebel vassal cycle"); this cycle was concerned with rebels against (often unjust) royal authority and its most famous characters were Renaud de Montauban and Girart de Roussillon.

   a) *Gormond et Isembart*

   b) *Girart de Roussillon* (1160-1170)

   c) *Renaud de Montauban* or *Les Quatre Fils Aymon* (end of the 12th century)

   d) *Raoul de Cambrai* (end of the 12th century)

   e) *Doon de Mayence* (mid 13th century)

4) A fourth grouping, not listed by Bertrand, is the Crusade cycle, dealing with the First Crusade and its immediate aftermath, and including:

   a) *Chanson d'Antioche*

   b) *Les Chetifs*

New *chansons* tended to be produced and incorporated into the existing literature in two ways:

1) A separate period or adventure in the life of an established hero was told (for example, his childhood).

2) The adventures of one of the ancestors or descendants of an established hero was told.

This method of epic expansion, with its obsession with blood line, was to be an important compositional technique throughout the Middle Ages. It also underscores the symbolic weight placed within this culture on family honor, paternal fidelity and on the idea of proving one's filial worth.

As the genre matured, it began to borrow elements from the French *roman* and the role of love became increasingly important. In some *chansons de geste* an element of self-parody appears, as in the Pelerinage de Charlemagne.

The Roman

Jean Bodel's other two categories—the "Matter of Rome" and the "Matter of Britain"—concern the French romance or "roman". The term "roman" signifies, roughly, "vernacular" (i.e. not Latin), but it is used to designate narrative poetry ("romance") usually written in octosyllabic rhymed couplets and telling stories of chivalry and love.

The most famous "romans" are those of the "Matter of Britain" dealing with Arthurian romance, the stories of Tristan and Iseult, the heroic legend of the doomed utopia of Camelot and the Holy Grail. Much of this material derives from Breton (Celtic) legends. The most important of these writers was Chrétien de Troyes (twelfth century).

The "Matter of Rome" concerns romances that take place in the ancient world, such as romances dealing with Alexander the Great, Troy, the Aeneid and Oedipus. Yet Bodel's category leaves little place for another important group of romances: those adventurous romances which are often set in Byzantium.

Sometimes linked with the "roman" are the *Breton lais,* narrative ballads of Britain by Marie de France, many of which have Celtic themes and origins.

From the 13th century on, verse romances were increasingly replaced by prose romances, and important verse romances of the 12th century were transformed into prose versions. It was chiefly in their prose form that romances were read from the 14th to the 16th century.

Important "Matter of Rome" romances of the 12th century:

1) *Roman de Thebés*
2) *Roman d'Eneas* (1160)
3) *Roman de Troie* (1154-1173)—Benoit de Sainte-Maure
4) *Roman d'Alexandre* (1177)—this romance uses a twelve-syllable verse and is the reason why this verse length is termed alexandrine

Important Byzantine and adventure romances of the 12th century:

1) *Flore and Blanchefleur*
2) *Florimont*—Aimon de Varenne (1188)
3) *Guillaume d'Angleterre*—sometimes ascribed to Chrétien de Troyes
4) *Robert le Diable*

Important romances of Britain of the 12th and 13th centuries:

1) *Brut*—Wace
2) *Erec and Enide*—Chrétien de Troyes
3) *Cliges*—Chretien de Troyes (1162)
4) *Lancelot" or "Lancelot, the Knight of the Cart*—Chrétien de Troyes (1164)
5) *Yvain, the Knight of the Lion*—Chrétien de Troyes (1180)

6) *Perceval* or the *Story of the Grail*—Chrétien de Troyes (1185)
7) *Romance of the Grail*—Robert de Boron (1191-1201)
8) *Tristan*—Thomas of Britain (1155-1178)
9) *Tristan*—Beroul (c.1190)
10) *Roman de Fergus*—William the Clerk (late 1100s/early 1200s)

Important romances of the 13th and 14th centuries:

1) *Chastelaine de Vergy*
2) The "Lancelot-Grail" or "Vulgate Cycle" and its sections - a prose reworking of the Lancelot and Grail stories (1205)
3) The "Post-Vulgate Cycle"—another prose reworking of the Lancelot and Grail stories
4) *Perceforest*
5) *Gui de Warewic* (1232-1242)
6) *Roman de la Rose* ("Romance of the Rose")—Guillaume de Lorris (around 1225-1237) and Jean de Meun (1266-1277)

The most important romance of the 13th century is the Romance of the Rose which breaks considerably from the conventions of the chivalric adventure story: in a dream a lover comes upon a garden and meets various allegorical figures. The second part of the work (written by Jean de Meun) expands on the initial material with scientific and mythological discussions. The novel would have an enormous impact on French literature up to the Renaissance.

Related to the previous romance is the medieval narrative poem called "dit" (literally "spoken", i.e. a poem not meant to be sung) which follows the poetic form of the "roman" (octosyllabic rhymed couplets). These first-person narrative works (which sometimes include inserted lyric poems) often use allegorical dreams (*songes*), allegorical characters, and the situation of the narrator-lover attempting to return toward or satisfy his lady. The 14th century poet Guillaume de Machaut is the most famous writers of "dits". King René I of Naples's allegorical romance *Cœur d'amour épris* (celebrated for its illustrations) is also a work in the same tradition.

Lyric Poetry

Medieval French lyric poetry was indebted to the poetic and cultural traditions in Southern France and Provence— including Toulouse, Poitiers, and the Aquitaine region—where "langue d'oc" was spoken (Occitan language); in their turn, the Provençal poets were greatly influenced by poetic traditions from the Hispano-Arab world. The Occitan or Provençal poets were called troubadours, from the word "trobar" (to find, to invent). Lyric poets in Old French are called "trouveres", using the Old French version of the word.

The occitan troubadours were amasingly creative in the development of verse forms and poetic genres, but their greatest impact on medieval literature was perhaps in their elaboration of complex code of love and service called "fin amors" or, more generally, courtly love. The "fin amors" tradition appears at roughly the same time in Europe as the Cult of the Virgin Mary, and the two have obvious similarities. In the "fin amors" tradition, the poet pledges his service to his lady ("dame", usually a married woman), in much the same way a knight or vassal pledges service to his lord. In the poems of the troubadours, the lady is frequently cold, distant, or upset with the poet and demands that he prove his service to her; the poet, for his part, is generally tormented by his passion, and his poems are often desperate pleas to his lady so that she might grant him some favor. In some troubadour poetry, the "favor" sought for is decidedly sexual, but in others there is a rarefied notion of love as spiritual and moral force.

Selected trouvere poets of the 12th and 13th centuries:

1) Conon de Bethune (c.1150-c.1219)
2) Le Chatelain de Couci (d.1203)
3) Blondel de Nesle (second half of the 12th century)
4) Richard the Lionheart (Richard Coeur de Lion) (1157-1199)
5) Gace Brule (active 1180-1213)
6) Colin Muset (around 1230)
7) Theobald IV of Champagne (1201-1253)
8) Adam de la Halle (c.1240-c.1288)
9) Guiot de Provins (d. after 1208)

By the late 13th century, the poetic tradition in France had begun to develop in ways that differed significantly from the troubadour poets, both in content and in the use of certain fixed forms. The new poetic (as well as musical: some of the earliest medieval music has lyrics composed in Old French by the earliest composers known by name) tendencies are apparent in the *Roman de Fauvel* in 1310 and 1314, a satire on abuses in the medieval church filled with medieval motets, lais, rondeaux and other new secular forms of poetry and music (mostly anonymous, but with several pieces by Philippe de Vitry who would coin the expression *Ars nova* [new art, or new technique] to distinguish the new musical practice from the music of the immediately preceding age). The best-known poet and composer of *ars nova* secular music and chansons was Guillaume de Machaut. (For more on music, medieval music; for more on music in the period after Machaux, Renaissance music).

Selected French poets from the late 13th to the 15th centuries:

1) Rutebeuf (d.1285)
2) Guillaume de Machaut (1300-1377)
3) Eustache Deschamps (1346-c.1406)
4) Alain Chartier (c. 1392 -c. 1430)
5) Christine de Pisan (1364-1430)
6) Charles, duc d'Orleans (1394-1465)
7) François Villon (1431-1465)

The last three poets on this list deserve further comment.

Charles, duc d'Orleans was a noble and head of one of the most powerful families in France during the Hundred Years' War. Captured in the Battle of Agincourt, he was a prisoner of the English from 1415-1441 and his ballades often speak of loss and isolation. His son became King Louis XII of France.

Christine de Pisan was one of the most prolific writers of her age; her "Cité des Dames" is considered a kind of "feminist manifesto".

Francois Villon was a student and vagabond whose two poetic "testaments" or "wills" are celebrated for their portrayal of the urban and university environment of Paris and their scabrous wit, satire and verbal puns. The image of Villon as vagabond poet seems to have gained almost mythic status in the 16th century, and this figure would be championed by poetic rebels of the 19th century and 20th centuries.

Poetic forms used by medieval French poets include:

1) Ballade
2) Rondeau (poetry) (or Rondel)
3) Ditie
4) Dits moraux
5) Lai
6) Virelai
7) Pastourelle
8) Complainte
9) Chanson
    a) Chanson de toile ("weaving song")
    b) Chanson de croisade
    c) Chanson courtoise
    d) Rotrouenge

Theater

Discussions about the origins of non-religious theater ("théâtre profane")— both drama and farce—in the Middle Ages remain controversial, but the idea of a continuous popular tradition stemming from Latin comedy and tragedy to the 9th century seems unlikely.

Most historians place the origin of medieval drama in the church's liturgical dialogues and "tropes". At first simply dramatisations of the ritual, particularly in those rituals connected with Christmas and Easter (*Mystery play*), plays were eventually transferred from the monastery church to the chapter house or refectory hall and finally to the open air, and the vernacular was substituted for Latin. In the 12th century one finds the earliest extant passages in French appearing as refrains inserted into liturgical dramas in Latin, such as a Saint Nicholas (patron saint of the student clercs) play and a Saint Stephen play.

Dramatic plays in French from the 12th and 13th centuries:

1) Le Jeu d'Adam (1150-1160)--written in octosyllabic rhymed couplets with Latin stage directions (implying that it was written by Latin-speaking clerics for a lay public)
2) Le Jeu de Saint Nicolas—Jean Bodel—written in octosyllabic rhymed couplets
3) Le Miracle de Theophile—Rutebeuf (c.1265)

The origins of farce and comic theater remain equally controversial; some literary historians believe in a non-liturgical origin (among "jongleurs" or in pagan and folk festivals), others see the influence of liturgical drama (some of the dramas listed above include farcical sequences) and monastic readings of Plautus and Latin comic theater.

Non-dramatic plays from the 12th and 13th centuries:

1) Le Dit de l'herberie—Rutebeuf
2) Courtois d'Arras (c.1228)
3) Le Jeu de la feuillé (1275)—Adam de la Halle
4) Le Jeu de Robin et de Marion (a pastourelle) (1288) —Adam de la Halle

5) Le Jeu du Pelerin (1288)
6) Le Garçon et l'aveugle (1266-1282)
7) Aucassin et Nicolette (a chantefable)—a mixture of prose and lyrical passages

Select list of plays from the 14th and 15th centuries:

1) La Farce de maitre Trubert et d'Antrongnard—Eustache Deschamps
2) Le Dit des quatre offices de l'ostel du roy—Eustache Deschamps
3) Miracles de Notre Dame
4) Bien Avise et mal avise (morality) (1439)
5) La Farce de maitre Pierre Pathelin (1464-1469)—this play had a great influence on Rabelais in the 16th century
6) Le Franc archer de Bagnolet (1468-1473)
7) Moralite (1486)—Henri Baude
8) L'Homme pecheur (morality) (1494)
9) La Farce du cuvier
10) La Farce nouvelle du pate et de la tarte

In the 15th century, the public representation of plays was organised and controlled by a number of professional and semi-professional guilds:

1) Clercs de la Basoche (Paris)—Morality plays
2) Enfants sans Souci (Paris)—Farces and Sotties
3) Conards (Rouen)
4) Confrerie de la Passion (Paris)—Mystery plays

Genres of theater practiced in the Middle Ages in France:

1) Farce—a realistic, humorous, and even coarse satire of human failings
2) Sottie—generally a conversation among idiots ("sots"), full of puns and quidproquos
3) Pastourelle—a play with a pastoral setting
4) Chantefable—a mixed verse and prose form only found in "Aucassin et Nicolette"
5) Mystery play—a depiction of the Christian mysteries or Saint's lives
6) Morality play
7) Miracle play
8) Passion play
9) Sermon Joyeux—a burlesque sermon

Other Forms

A large body of fables survive in Old French; these include (mostly anonymous) literature dealing with the recurring trickster character of Reynard the Fox. Marie de France was also active in this genre, producing the *Ysopet* (Little Aesop) series of fables in verse.

Related to the fable was the more bawdy "fabliau", which covered topics such as cuckolding and corrupt clergy. These "fabliaux" would be an important source for Chaucer and for the Renaissance short story ("conte" or "nouvelle").

Satire was also written during this period, including the *Roman de Fauvel*, which mocks the sins of humanity by making the Seven Deadly Sins appear in the personification of a horse.

The prose satire *Les XV [Quinze] joies de mariage* (*The Fifteen Joys of Marriage*, first published 1480-90, written perhaps in the early 15th century, and attributed variously to Antoine de la Sale, Gilles Bellemere the bishop of Avignon, and many others) is a riotous critique of wives (typical of misogynistic literature of the period), but it also provides important insight into the economic and social life of a married household in the 15th century.

Prose compositions in the Middle Ages—other than the prose versions of romances and "chansons de geste"—include a number of histories and chronicles, of which the most famous are those of Robert de Clari and Geoffroy de Villehardouin (both on the Fourth crusade of 1204 and the capture of Constantinople), Jean de Joinville (on Saint Louis IX of France), Jean Froissart (on the wars of the 14th century) and Philippe de Commines and Enguerrand de Monstrelet (on the troubles of the 15th century). Philippe de Mezieres wrote "Songe du Vieil Pelerin" (1389), an elaborate allegorical voyage in which he described the customs of Europe and the near East.

4

Medieval German Literature

Medieval German literature refers to literature written in Germany, stretching from the Carolingian dynasty; various dates have been given for the end of the German literary Middle Ages, the Reformation (1517) being the last possible cut-off point.

Old High German Period (800–1100)

The oldest known literary work in German is the epic *Hildebrandslied* (Lay of Hildebrand), which survives in a fragment dating from about ad 800. This work describes, in mixed Low and High German alliterative verse, the confrontation and the beginning of a battle between the legendary hero Hildebrand and his son. Other legends deal with such heroic personalities as Theodoric, king of the Ostrogoths; Attila, king of the Huns; and Siegfried, identified by some authorities as the German chief Arminius, who defeated the Romans in the Teutoburger Wald, a forest in Lower Saxony in ad 9.

This pagan tradition was disowned by the Roman Catholic church, which remained the dominant force in German literature from the 4th to the 12th century. As early as 381 Ulfilas, bishop of the Goths, translated the

Bible into the vernacular, and an anonymous priest wrote *Muspilli,* an alliterative poem in Bavarian dialect depicting the destruction of the world by fire on Judgment Day. Another important work, written in the old Low German dialect, is the epic *Heliand,* in which Christ is represented as a German prince with feudal retainers as his disciples.

Under the Frankish ruler Charles Martel and his successors, many abbeys were founded, among them the famous Sankt Gallen and Fulda in Germany. In these abbeys the monks preserved ancient literature as well as the history of their own time. During this period, however, the major literary works were written in Latin, with German being used primarily in translations from the older language. An example of an epic written in Latin is the *Walthariusleid* by Ekkehard I the Elder of Sankt Gallen, which tells of the escape of the hero Walter and his bride from the court of Attila. In addition to such epics, written for the royal courts, a popular oral literature developed during the 9th and 10th centuries. It consisted largely of tales and ballads, which were not written down until about the 14th century.

Epic Poetry

The most famous work in OHG is the *Hildebrandslied,* a short piece of Germanic alliterative heroic verse which besides the *Muspilli* is the sole survivor of what must have been a vast oral tradition. Another important work, in the northern dialect of Old Saxon, is a life of Christ in the style of a heroic epic known as the *Heliand.*

Hildebrandslied

The opening lines of the poem set the scene: two

warriors meet on a battlefield, probably as the champions of their two armies. As the older man, Hildebrand opens by asking the identity and genealogy of his opponent. Hadubrand reveals that he did not know his father but the elders told him his father was Hildebrand, who fled eastwards in the service of Dietrich (Theodoric) to escape the wrath of Otacher (Odoacer), leaving behind a wife and small child. He believes his father to be dead.

Hildebrand responds by saying that Hadubrand will never fight such a close kinsman (an indirect way of asserting his paternity) and offers gold arm-rings he had received as a gift from the Lord of the Huns (the audience would have recognized this as a reference to Attila, whom according to legend Theodoric served).

Hadubrand takes this as a ruse to get him off guard and belligerently refuses the offer, accusing Hildebrand of deception, and perhaps implying cowardice. Hildebrand accepts his fate and sees that he cannot honourably refuse battle: he has no choice but to kill his own son or be killed by him. They start to fight, and the text concludes with their shields smashed. But the poem breaks off, not revealing the outcome.

The text consists of 68 lines of alliterative verse, though written continuously with no indication the verse form. It breaks off in mid-line, leaving the poem unfinished at the end of the second page. However, it does not seem likely that much more than a dozen lines are missing.

The text is highly problematic, both because of the circumstances of its transmission and because of the uniqueness of the work. Although the written text presents no gaps, a number of places have been identified where the text appears not to follow or there are incomplete lines of verse, suggesting missing text. Other apparent illogicalities suggest misattributed direct speech and lines out of order, though these remain matters of debate.

While it has always been accepted that the text derives ultimately from an oral original, it is unlikely that the surviving text was transcribed directly from oral performance, or indeed written down by someone competent in the oral tradition. The transpositions, apparent lacunae, and unwarranted insertions all indicate a text copied from an earlier manuscript by scribes with only a partial understanding of the poetic form. The mixture of dialects and other linguistic oddities found in the text could also indicate that the poem was intentionally written to appear to be older than it was.

The manuscript of the *Hildebrandslied* is now in the Murhardsche Bibliothek in Kassel and was discovered around 1715 by Johan Georg von Eckert. It is assumed to derive, like much else in the library's collection, from the monastery of Fulda.

It is written on two leaves of parchment, the first and last in a theological codex. The codex itself was written in the first quarter of the 9th century, with the text of the *Hildebrandslied* added in the 830s on the two remaining blank leaves. There is no evidence to support the suggestion of a missing third leaf which would have contained the end of the poem.

The manuscript is the work of two scribes, of whom the second wrote only 11 lines at the beginning of the second leaf. The hand is mainly Carolingian minuscule. A number of features, including the *wynn*-rune used for *w* suggest Old English influence, not surprising in a house founded by Anglo-Saxon missionaries.

The manuscript pages now show a number of patches of discoloration. These are the results of attempts by earlier scholars to improve the legibility of the text with chemical agents.

At the end of the Second World War the codex went missing, looted by a US army officer and sold into the rare book trade. It was eventually discovered in California and returned to Kassel in 1955. However, the first sheet had been cut out by ignorant antiquars, and it was only in 1972 that this was rediscovered in Philadelphia and returned. Further damage had been done to this leaf in order to help disguise its origin.

One of the most puzzling features of the *Hildebrandslied* is its dialect, which is a mixture of Old Bavarian and Old Saxon. For example, the first person pronoun appears both in the Old Saxon form *ik* and the Old High German *ih*. The reason for the dialect mixture is unknown, but it seems certain it cannot have been the work of the last scribes and was already present in the original which they copied.

The Old Saxon features predominate in the opening part of the poem and show a number of errors, which argue against an Old Saxon original. The alliteration of *riche* and *reccheo* in line 48 is often regarded as conclusive: the equivalent Old Saxon forms, do not alliterate and would have given a malformed line. Earlier scholars envisaged an Old Saxon original, but an Old High German original is now universally accepted.

The East Franconian dialect of Fulda was High German, but the monastery was a centre of missionary activity to Northern Germany. It is therefore not unreasonable to assume there was some knowledge of Old Saxon there, and perhaps even some Old Saxon speakers. However, the motivation for attempting a translation into Old Saxon remains inscrutable, and attempts to link it with Fulda's missionary activity among the Saxons remain speculative.

An alternative explanation treats the dialect as homogeneous, interpreting it as representative of an archaic poetic idiom.

Although the ending is missing, later works which draw on the same legendary material offer evidence about the original conclusion:

- In the 13th century Old Norse Thiðrekssaga, Hildibrand defeats his son, Alibrand. Alibrand offers his sword in surrender but attempts to strike Hildibrand as he reaches for it. Hildibrand taunts him for having been taught to fight by a woman, but then asks if he is Alibrand and they are reconciled.
- The Middle High German *Jüngeres Hildebrandslied* (probably 13th Century) tells a similar story of the treacherous blow, the taunt that the son was taught to fight by a woman, and the final reconciliation.
- In the 14th century Old Norse *Ásmundar saga kappabana,* Hildebrand's shield bears paintings of the warriors he has killed, which include his own son.
- In the Faroese ballad *Snjólvskvæði,* Hildebrand is tricked into killing his son.
- In Book VII of the *Gesta Danorum* (early 13th century), Hildiger reveals as he is dying that he has killed his own son.

Even though some of these versions end in reconciliation, this can be seen as a concession to the courtly tastes of a later period. The heroic ethos of an earlier period would leave Hildebrand no choice but to kill his son after the treacherous stroke, and this is preserved in the other analogues.

A more distant analogue is the Persian tale of Rostam in the Shahnameh (*The Epic of Kings*), who kills his son Sohrab in single combat between two armies. They do not recognize each other until, after Sohrab has been fatally wounded, Rostam sees the arm-ring he had given his son at his birth. The similarities with the *Hildebrandslied* suggest the story may derive from a Proto-Indo-European folk tale.

Although there is no evidence that Hildebrand himself was a historical character, the background to the poem is formed by historical events in 6th century Italy, where the Ostrogothic King Theodoric fought for mastery of Italy against Odoacer, the Germanic general who had deposed the Romulus Augustulus. Theodoric appears widely in Germanic legend as Dietrich von Bern (Verona).

Theodoric's Gothic Kingdom of Italy was subsequently seized by the Lombards, who had close connections with the Bavarians in South Germany, both speaking closely related Upper German dialects. This accounts for the transmission of legendary material relating to Theodoric northwards. Even if the Scandinavian analogues did not suggest wider dissemination, the close links between Bavaria and Fulda - the first abbot Sturmi was a member of the Bavarian nobility - would in any case be sufficient to account for knowledge of this material in the monastery.

Muspilli

Muspilli is one of but two surviving pieces of Old High German epic poetry (the other being *Hildebrandslied*), dating to around 870. One large fragment of the text has survived in the margins and empty pages of a codex marked as the possession of Louis the German and now in the Bayerische Staatsbibliothek. The beginning and end of the poem have not survived. It was re-discovered in 1817 and first published in 1832 by Johann Andreas Schmeller, who also titled it *Muspilli,* after a central word in the text.

The poem has been theorized as a Christianized version of the pagan Ragnarök, with figures represented in 13th century sources swapped with Christian figures; Surtr replaced by the Antichrist whom Elias - replacing Thor - fights, Loki by the old fiend. In the Norse Ragnarök, Muspelheim and Muspel play a large role, and both versions involve a wolf. Grau proposes a connection of all of the material in the poem except for two verses to the 4th century theologian Ephraim the Syrian.

The etymology and meaning of the term *Muspilli* (a hapax legomenon in Old High German, though forms of the word are attested in Old Saxon and Old Norse) is uncertain, but it is surmised to describe some sort of cataclysmic end of the world in fire (*ekpyrosis*). The poem is an example of early Germanic Christianity, combining pagan elements with the Biblical or Christian concepts, featuring Elijah, the Antichrist and the Last Judgement. Muspel and Muspil translate as "Muor's" "Maris" "Marsh" Pfell. Where Fell is the Norse word for Hill. What they are describing is a lighthouse possibly also a smithery burning on a hill at the edge of the sea. It may be a referenc to Pfellwyorm. If you have ever been out to sea in a small ship you would understand what it is like to be between heaven and hell.

The focus of the text is first on the fate of the soul after death. The hosts of heaven and hell do battle over the deceased individual's soul and the winning party will carry it off as booty. Attention then shifts to another battle, the battle between Elijah and the Antichrist, which the text says will precede the Last Judgement. The two combatants are fighting as champions for God and the Devil, respectively. The Antichrist will fall but Elijah will be wounded and his blood dripping on the Earth will set the world on fire – announcing the *muspilli*. The rest of the poem is concerned with the Resurrection and Judgment Day itself.

Lyric Poetry

Works include the short but splendid *Ludwigslied*, celebrating the victory of the Frankish army, led by Louis III of France, over Danish (Viking) raiders at the Battle of Saucourt-en-Vimeu on 3 August 881. There is also the incomplete *Das Georgslied* about the life of Saint George, and the Wessobrunn Prayer, a praise of Creation and a plea for strength to withstand sin.

Ludwigslied

The *Ludwigslied* (in English, *Lay* or *Song of Ludwig*) is an Old High German poem of 59 rhyming couplets, celebrating the victory of the Frankish army, led by Louis III of France, over Danish (Viking) raiders at the Battle of Saucourt-en-Vimeu on 3 August 881.

The poem is thoroughly Christian in ethos. It presents the Viking raids as a punishment from God:

He caused the Northmen to come across the see to remind the Frankish people of their sins, and inspired Louis to ride to the aid of his people. Louis praises God both before and after the battle.

Although the poem is Christian in content, and the use of rhyme reflects Christian rather than Germanic poetic tradition, it is not without Germanic elements. It belongs to the genre of *Preislied,* a song in praise of a warrior, of a type which must have been common in Germanic oral tradition.

The poem is preserved in over four pages in a single 9th century manuscript formerly in the monastery of Saint-Amand, now in the Bibliothèque municipale, Valenciennes (Codex 150, f. 141v-143r). In the same manuscript, and written by the same scribe, is the Old French Sequence of Saint Eulalia.

The poem speaks of Louis in the present tense: it opens, "I know a king called Ludwig who willingly serves God. I know he will reward him for it". Since Louis died in August the next year, the poem must have been written within a year of the battle. However, in the manuscript, the poem is headed *Ritmus teutonicus de piae memoriae Hluduice rege* (*German song to the beloved memory of King Louis*), which means it must be a copy of an earlier text.

The dialect of the poem generally regarded as Rhine Franconian, though there are some peculiarities which have received a variety of explanations. It is assumed that the manuscript was written by a bilingual scribe in Saint-Amand and we have no other example of an OHG text from this area. Some regard it as the sole textual example of the otherwise little known West Franconian dialect, which is assumed to have been the language of the Carolingian court.

Das Georgslied

The George Song is Old High German poetry, emerged towards the end of the 9th Jahrhunderts. Century. In eine Handschrift des ersten namentlich bekannten althochdeutschen Dichters Otfrid von Weißenburg trug an der Wende zum oder am Beginn des 11. In a manuscript of the first Old High German poet known by name Otfrid of Wissembourg was at the turn or at the beginning of the 11th Jahrhunderts ein unbekannter Schreiber die althochdeutsche Dichtung des Georgsliedes ein. Century, an unknown writer, the Old High German poetry of Georg song book.

Perhaps the Georgslied reaches the end of the 9th Jahrhunderts zurück, vielleicht ging der Verschriftlichung des Liedes eine längere mündliche Überlieferung voraus, vielleicht existierte aber auch eine schriftliche Vorlage. Centuries back, perhaps preceded the transcript of the song a long oral tradition, but perhaps there was also a written submission. Mitunter wurde eine Verfasserschaft des Dichters Otfrid erwogen. Sometimes a poet's authorship of the Otfrid was considered.

The classification of the George song in the general context of early medieval Georg worship is the (historical and germanistische) medieval studies disagree. Die althochdeutsche Georgsdichtung könnte im Eifelkloster Prüm entstanden sein. The Old High German Georg seal could have originated in the Eifel Monastery Prüm. Das karolingische Hauskloster hatte im Jahr 852 von Kaiser Lothar I. (840–855), dem älteren Bruder Ludwigs des Deutschen, eine Armreliquie des kappadokischen Heiligen erhalten.

The Carolingian family monastery had received in the year 852 I, Emperor Lothair (840-855), the older brother of Louis the German, a Armreliquie the Cappadocian saints. Damit wurde Prüm zu einem Zentrum der ostfränkischen Georgsverehrung. Thus Prüm was a center of the East Frankish Georg worship. Doch auch eine Entstehung des Georgsliedes in Schwaben bzw. auf der Reichenau scheint nicht ausgeschlossen. But even a rise of George song in Swabia and on the Reichenau is not impossible. Durch den Mainzer Erzbischof und Reichenauer Abt Hatto III. (891–913) gelangten Georgsreliquien nach Schwaben, u. a. By the Archbishop of Mainz and Reichenau Abbot Hatto III. (891-913) George relics came to Swabia, and Others das Georgshaupt zur Georgskirche in Reichenau-Oberzell (896). the "George Main," to George's Church in Reichenau-Obernzell (896).

Middle High German Period (1100–1370)

Although prose writing and drama were found primarily in the form of didactic religious works throughout the Middle High German period, poetry developed as a mode of secular expression, and epic, lyric, and satiric forms appeared, giving voice to the virtues of chivalry and courtly love. The *Spielleute,* or wandering minstrels, entertained their listeners with stories of adventure sometimes based on the experiences of warriors returning from the Crusades. Among the epic poems of the period, *König Rother* had the greatest success. Another important style was the court epic, which reached its highest form in the works of Hartmann von Aue, Gottfried von Strassburg, Wolfram von Eschenbach, and Heinrich von Veldeke (fl. about 1160–1200). Although the works of such French writers as Chrétien de Troyes and others served as models for the German epics, the German writers expressed their own ideals, found their own form and style, and very often added depth to the stories. A variation of the court epic was the epic in which an animal was the central figure. *Reinecke Fuchs* by Heinrich der Glîchezaere is the best example. The greatest of the German epics is the NIBELUNGENLIED, set down in the early 13th century by an unknown author.

Lyric poetry during the Middle High German period developed in the form of the *Minnesang,* or courtly lyric, composed by the lyric poets known as MINNESINGER. The great master of this type of poetry is Walther von der Vogelweide. His works, which include love songs, religious lyrics, and epigrams, express personal and political idealism and assert his independence of papal authority.

In the second half of the 13th century the nature of the epic began to change as characters from the middle class and the peasantry were introduced. The peasantry, once an object of derision, became increasingly important in literature, figuring prominently in such works as *Meier Helmbrecht,* a 13th-century tale of peasant life.

Epic Poetry

The *Kaiserchronik* is one of the first monuments of Middle High German. The three key authors of courtly romances are Hartmann von Aue, Gottfried von Strassburg, and Wolfram von Eschenbach, in particular his *Parzival,* which is regarded as one of the supreme literary achievements of the period. The revamping of the heroic tradition is visible in works like the *Nibelungenlied* and *Kudrun.* Another epic of the High Middle Ages is *Herzog Ernst;* other authors include

Konrad von Wurzburg, Rudolf von Ems, and Ulrich von Türheim.

Kaiserchronik

The *Kaiserchronik* (*Der Keiser und der Kunige buoch,* "the book of emperors and kings") is a 12th century German epic poem. It is at once a kind ot "Legend of all the Saints" and a confused but remarkable account of the Roman emperors and also of the German emperors and kings up to the crusade of King Conrad III (1147). The language is comparatively good and often quite poetic.

The chronicle was written about 1150. Undoubtedly the work of an ecclesiastic of Ratisbon, an earnest partisan of the Guelphs, the chronicle is not improbably to be referred to Konrad der Pfaffe, who composed the well-known "Song of Roland" (*Rolandslied*). He drew his information from the *Chronicon Wirzeburgense,* the *Chronicle of Ekkehard,* and the *Annolied;* it may be that he also drew from some earlier record or rhymed chronicle. Judging from the large number of manuscripts still extant (twelve complete and seventeen partial), it must have been very popular, and it was twice continued in the 13th century.

The original poem, according to modern authorities, ended with verse 17283; the first addition, called "Bavarian", comprised 800 verses, while the second, the "Swabian", which brought the poem to the Interregnum (1254–73), consisted of 483 lines. The chronicle was first published in full by Massmann, with careful researches into manuscripts, investigation of authorship, age, etc. The best edition is that of Schröder.

Parzival

Parzival is a major medieval German epic poem by the poet Wolfram von Eschenbach, in the Middle High German language. The poem, commonly dated to the first quarter of the 13th century, is itself largely based on Chrétien de Troyes's *Perceval, the Story of the Grail* and mainly centers on the Arthurian hero Parzival (Percival in English) and his long quest for the Holy Grail following his initial failure to achieve it.

As in the extant copies of Chretien's tale a long section is devoted to Parzival's friend Gawan and his adventures defending himself from a false murder charge and winning the hand of the maiden Orgeluse. The poem continues to be read and translated into modern languages around the world. Among the most striking elements of the text are the scope of its plot and its emphasis on the virtues of compassion and spiritual questing.

The poem was widely influential in Germany in the Middle Ages and beyond. Wolfram himself began a prequel, *Titurel,* which was later continued by another writer, while two full romances were written adapting Wolfram's story of Loherangrin. Richard Wagner based his famous opera *Parsifal,* finished in 1883, on *Parzival.*

Parzival is divided into sixteen books, each composed of several thirty-line stanzas of rhyming couplets. The stanza lengths fit perfectly onto a manuscript page. For the subject matter Wolfram von Eschenbach relied on the Grail romance, *Perceval, the Story of the Grail,* left incomplete by Chrétien de Troyes. Wolfram claimed that a certain Kyot the Provençal supplied additional material drawn from

Arabic and Angevin sources but this is not taken seriously by most scholars.

Plot

Parzival's heroic traits are (eventually) his empathy and wisdom, ultimately manifested in his final attempt to heal Anfortas, the Fisher King. Parzival is described by the author as "a brave man, slowly wise". His initial flaws are his youthful ignorance and selfishness, as when he abandons his heartbroken mother to become a knight or when he conceives God as a sort of feudal overlord.

Book I opens with the death of King Gandin, Parzival's grandfather. His oldest son, Galoes, receives the kingdom but offers his brother Gahmuret the land of Anjou in fief. However, Gahmuret departs to gain renown. He travels to the African kingdom of Zazamanc, whose capital is under siege from two different armies. Gahmuret offers his services to the city, and his offer is accepted by Queen Belacane. He conquers the invaders, marries Queen Belacane, and becomes king of Zazamanc and Azagouc. Growing bored with peace, Gahmuret steals away on a ship, abandoning his pregnant wife. Belacane later gives birth to a son, Feirefiz (whose skin is mottled black and white).

In Book II, Gahmuret returns to the West, where he meets and marries Queen Herzeloyde. Ever restless, however, he soon returns to fight for the Baruch in the Far East, where he is later killed by a treacherous acquaintance.

Book III tells of how the pregnant Herzeloyde, grief-stricken at her husband's death, retires to a secluded forest dwelling and vows to protect her new child, Parzival, from the ways of knighthood at all costs by raising him entirely ignorant of chivalry and the ways of men. His seclusion is shattered by four knights passing who tell him of King Arthur's court at Camelot. Enamored, he decides to go join Arthur's court. His mother is heartbroken at the news of his decision but allows him to depart, dressing him in fool's garments in the hopes that the knights will refuse to take him in. Soon after his departure she dies, utterly bereft.

The first part of the journey takes place completely in the world of King Arthur, where the colourful and strange appearance of Parzival awakens the interest of the court. After becoming entangled in courtly intrigue between Duke Orilus and his wife Jeschute he meets his cousin Sigune who reveals to him his true name. Parzival also fights and kills Ither, the red knight of Kukumerlant. Putting on the red knight's armor he rides away from the court and meets Gurnemanz, from whom he learns the duties of a knight, especially self-control and moderation. Gurnemanz also advises him to avoid impudent curiosity.

In Book IV Parzival meets and falls in love with the maiden Condwiramurs when he lends his aid to her town, which is under siege. They marry but he leaves soon afterwards to seek news of his mother.

In Book V he arrives at the castle of the Grail. He does not ask his host, the Fisher King Anfortas, about his mysterious wound, however, or about the magical objects paraded before him, remembering Gurnemanz's advice to be not too curious. The next morning Parzival finds himself completely alone in a totally deserted castle, leading him to speculate that his experiences of the previous night were an illusion conjured by malevolent spirits to snare him.

Parzival returns to the world of Arthur and again meets Sigune, who now explains to him that his mother Herzeloyde is the sister of the dangerously ill Anfortas, king of the grail. He also meets Jeschute again, who was unwittingly humiliated by him the last time, and defeats Orilus in single combat. Eventually Parzival renews the marriage of Jeschute and Orilus.

Parzival returns in Book VI as a perfect potential member of the Round Table to King Arthur. But during a festive meal, Cundrie, messenger of the grail, appears, curses Parzival in the name of the grail and claims that Parzival had lost his honour. Parzival immediately leaves the court even though he is not able to understand his guilt.

Gawan takes over as the central figure of Books VII-VIII as he tries to clear his name of a false charge of murder.

In Book IX, we learn that Parzival fights for the good but suffers from his alienation from God. After nearly five years of wandering and fighting, from combat he gains a new horse, owned by a grail knight, and this horse leads him one Good Friday to Trevrizent to whom he introduces himself as a penitent sinner. He stays with this holy man for fourteen days and learns about the hidden meaning of life and the true meaning of the grail. He makes a step towards a life of spiritual understanding. Through his loneliness and through his yearning for the grail and for Condwiramurs he puts himself outside the world of Arthur. He is called to another world, that of the grail.

Books X-XIV tell of Gawan's attempts to win the hand of the maiden Orgeluse.

In Book XV, Parzival fights with a knight who is the first to seem more adept than he. Parzival's sword breaks but, instead of slaying him, the other knight sees no honor in such a feat and both retire to the grass. There they learn that they share the same father. "I was against my own self," says Parzival to Feirefiz, his brother from afar. Again Cundrie appears and proclaims now that Parzival's name has appeared on the grail, marking him as the new grail king.

During his journey to the grail in Book XVI Parzival reunites with his wife and takes Feirefiz as a companion. Feirefiz cannot see the grail, but he can see the grail maiden and promptly falls in love with her.

Some details of the epic have inspired controversy, partly because the narrative is interspersed with humorous anecdotes by Wolfram. It is not clear whether many of the claims he makes are intended to be taken as fact or as jest.

For example, in one passage he claims to be totally illiterate: whether the original poem was composed as part of an oral tradition or as a written work is a subject of debate among scholars. Wolfram also claimed that a lost Arabic manuscript by a descendant of Solomon was discovered by a certain Kyot the Provençal, though this may have been his way of parodying the dubious veracity of many other Grail texts.

Events in the main sequence of *Parzival* (excluding the narrative of Gahmuret) take place in what is now called Great Britain. There are difficulties in more specific identification, which pose some fundamental geographical problems; scholars both medieval and modern are divided as to whether or not many of the places visited by Parzival are real.

Kudrun

Kudrun (sometimes known as Gudrun Lied), is a Middle High German epic, written probably in the early years of the 13th century, not long after the Nibelungenlied, the influence of which may be traced upon it.

It is preserved in a single manuscript, which was prepared at the command of Maximilian I, and was discovered as late as 1820 in the Ambras Castle in Tirol. The author was an unnamed Austrian poet, but the story itself belongs to the cycle of sagas, which originated on the shores of the North Sea.

The epic falls into three easily distinguishable parts: the adventures of King Hagen of Ireland; the romance of Hettel, king of the Hegelingen, who woos and wins Hagen's daughter Hilde; and lastly the more or less parallel story of how Herwig, king of Seeland, wins Gudrun, the daughter of Hettel and Hilde, in opposition to her father's wishes. Gudrun is carried off by a king of Normandy, and her kinsfolk, who are in pursuit, are defeated in a great battle on the island of Wulpensand off the Dutch coast.

The finest parts of the epic are those in which Gudrun, a prisoner in the Norman castle, refuses to become the wife of her captor, and is condemned to do the most menial work of the household. Here, thirteen years later, Herwig and her brother Ortwin find her washing clothes by the sea; on the following day they attack the Norman castle with their army and carry out the long-delayed retribution.

The epic of Gudrun is not unworthy to stand beside the greater Nibelungenlied, and it has been aptly compared with it as the Odyssey to the Iliad. Like the Odyssey, Gudrun is an epic of the sea, a story of adventure; it does not turn solely round the conflict of human passions; nor is it built up around one all-absorbing, all-dominating idea as the Nibelungenlied is. Scenery and incident are more varied, and the poet has an opportunity for a more lyric interpretation of motive and character. Gudrun is composed in stanzas similar to those of the Nibelungenlied, but with the essential difference that the last line of each stanza is identical with the others, and does not contain the extra accented syllable characteristic of the Nibelungen metre.

Herzog Ernst

Herzog Ernst is a German epic from the early high Middle Ages (c. 1180), first written down by an anonymous author from the Rhein region.

The main theme of the story is an argument between a Bavarian duke (Herzog Ernst) and his stepfather Kaiser Otto I. The story is split into two parts:

— Ernst becomes a Herzog and, as a result of the malicious scheming of the Kaiser's uncle, Pfalzgraf Heinrich, is outlawed.

— Herzog Ernst travels through the Orient in search of the Holy Grave. He encounters wonderful things, for example, creatures with human bodies and bird's heads. Eventually, he decides to return home and tricks the Kaiser into forgiving him.

The epic blends together two historical events: an argument between Herzog Liudolf and his father Otto

I in 953-954; and the rebellion of Herzog Ernst II from Swabia (born 1007) against his stepfather King Konrad II in 1026-1027

This story was very popular in the Middle Ages in Germany, as evidenced by the number of manuscripts that have been found in a wide range of places. It was popular due to its fantastical descriptions of the Orient and far away lands (a popular topic due to the Second Crusade), and also its introduction of the concept of chivalry.

Herzog Ernst is usually grouped under the heading 'Spielmannsdichtung' or 'Spielmannsepos'. This term is used to describe a handful of other manuscripts of the time, due to the assumption that they were written and told by Spielmänner (a kind of jester). However, this term has recently been disputed, as these works are considered too complex to have been written by Spielmänner, who are generally thought to have been uneducated.

Lyric Poetry

The most impressive example of Early Middle High German literature is the *Annolied.* It was about the beginning of the 12th century that Ava became the first woman to write poetry in German. The "big name" of Minnesang is Walther von der Vogelweide, but there are many others, and some of their melodies have survived. Other notable works include the incomplete *Christherre-Chronik,* a 13th-century world chronicle from Thuringen, and the works of Heinrich Frauenlob.

Annolied

The Annolied (*"Song of Anno"*) was composed in about 1100 in Early Middle High German rhyming couplets by a monk of Siegburg Abbey. A principal point of reference for the dating is the mention of Mainz as a place of coronation. The German kings were usually crowned in Aachen, and the naming of Mainz in this connection most likely refers to the coronation either of the counter-king Rudolf of Rheinfelden in 1077 or that of Emperor Henry V in 1106.

The Annolied was an encomium to Bishop Anno II of Cologne (d. 1075), later Saint Anno, who was the founder of Siegburg Abbey.

The poem consists of three parts: the religious or spiritual history of the world and its salvation, from the creation to the time of Anno II; the secular history of the world up to the foundation of the German cities (including the theory of the world empires derived from the vision of the Book of Daniel); and finally the *"Vita Annonis"*, or the biography of Bishop Anno II.

A recent interpretation (Dunphy, Herweg) sees this threefold structure in the context of the poet's remark in the prologue that in the beginning God created two worlds, one spiritual and one earthly, and then he mixed these to create the first human, who, being both, was a "third world". The poem then charts spiritual and secular history and finally shows the two culminating in the biography of the man who stands at the centrepoint of history. This is a remarkable and highly original historiographical approach.

Parts of the Annolied were incorporated into the later Middle High German Kaiserchronik and the two works are often considered together.

Christherre-Chronik

The *Christherre-Chronik* (named after its opening words, "Christ the Lord") is a 13th-century world chronicle from Thüringen, written in Middle High German rhyming couplets. It was written by a churchman in the service of Henry III, Markgrave of Meissen, and may be seen as attempting a spiritual answer to the courtly world chronicle of Rudolf von Ems. The work begins with the creation of the world and was apparently intended to follow world history until the poet's own day, but it was never finished. It breaks off during the account of the book of judges, and in the manuscripts it is continued with text from other chronicles, including (ironically) that of Rudolf, and also sometimes the *Weltchronik* of Jans der Enikel. There is still no edition of this text. Excerpts with English translations can be found in: Graeme Dunphy (ed.), *History as Literature: German World Chronicles of the Thirteenth Century in Verse.* Kalamazoo 2003.

Urban Literature

From the later 13th century, the rise of urban literature, which becomes the dominant force from the mid-14th century onwards. This urbanisation and the introduction of printing in the 15th century are the main developments marking the very vague boundary between late medieval and early modern German literature.

Lyric Poetry

The first important urban author was the Viennese chronicler Jans der Enikel. Other poets include Hans Folz, Johannes von Tepl, and Sebastian Brant.

Jans der Enikel

Jans der Enikel, i.e. "Jans the Grandson" was a Viennese poet and historian of the late 13th century.

He wrote a *Weltchronik* (history of the world) and a *Fürstenbuch* (history of Vienna), both in Middle High German verse.

The *Weltchronik* tells the history of the world, starting even before the six-day creation by telling of Satan's rebellion in Heaven, and relating the Biblical stories of the Old Testament (oddly not the New), then continuing with Homer and other classical Greek and Roman material, and on down the list of Emperors through Charles the Great to Frederick II, Holy Roman Emperor.

The style is anecdotal, with many fun tales inserted into what might otherwise be sober history. For example, the reign of Frederick II is interrupted to tell an entirely fictional story of a nobleman named Friedrich von Antfurt. This Friedrich subjects a duchess to what we today could only call sexual harassment, to the point where she thinks up a ruse to get rid of him. She promises to give him what he wants (and the poet makes no bones about the fact that he only wants her body!) provided he takes part in a joust wearing her chemise (underdress) instead of his armour. She is of course counting on him being killed. But he survives, and there has to be a reckoning.

Jans is recorded in a number of Viennese documents for the years 1271-1302. He is known to have been a member of one of the highest patrician families of the city.

Hans Folz

Hans Folz (c. 1437–January 1513) was a notable medieval German author.Folz was born in Worms. He was made a citizen of the city of Nuremberg, Germany in 1459 and master barber of the city in 1486. Folz was a reformer of the meistersangs, adding 27 new tones to those that had been allowed by the twelve "Alten Meister" (old masters) up to that point. His *Meisterlieder* (a type of song), of which he wrote about a thousand, were mostly devoted to religious questions. He also wrote twelve *Fastnachtsspiele* (short plays that made light of people in medieval society, for instance farmers, priests, and the bourgeoisie) in the same style as Hans Rosenplüt, but with more subtle language.

Folz has been labelled as an anti-semite by Andrew Gow, who called him "a thorough-going Jew-hater" for his work *Ein Spil von dem Herzogen von Burgund* (*A Story of the Dukes of Burgund*). According to Albert Wimmer's *Anthology of Medieval German Literature,* "Folz's plays were trendsetters in the development of moderately dramatic plays (so-called «Handlungsspiele»)"

Johannes von Tepl

Johannes von Tepl (c. 1350 – c. 1415), also known as Johannes von Saaz (Czech: *Jan ze Žatce*), was a Bohemian writer of the German language, one of the earliest known writers of prose in Early New High German (or late Middle German—depending on the criteria).

Not much is known about him; historians presume that he probably studied at universities in Prague, Bologna and Padua. In 1383, he became a solicitor in Žatec (Saaz) and in 1386 a rector of the town's Latin school. From the year 1411 on, he lived in Prague. He spent almost all his life in the Bohemian kingdom during the reign of kings Charles and

Wenceslaus. Johannes von Tepl is best known for his early humanist poem *Der Ackermann aus Böhmen* (*Ploughman of Bohemia*), sometimes also called *Der Ackermann und der Tod* (*Ploughman and Death*), written around 1401 and first printed in 1460. It is a dialogue of Death and Ploughman, whose wife Margaretha recently died. Central themes of the book are their opposing views on life, mankind, and morality. (In the history of Bohemia, the ploughman is an important symbol of Bohemian kings — PYaemysl, the legendary founder of the PYaemyslid dynasty, was originally a ploughman.) The poem is regarded as one of the most important German poems in the late Middle Ages.

Sebastian Brant

Sebastian Brant (also Brandt) (1457 - 10 May 1521) was an Alsatian humanist and satirist. He was born in Strasbourg. He studied at Basel, took the degree of doctor of law in 1489, and for some time held a professorship of jurisprudence there. Returning to Strasbourg, he was made syndic of the town, remaining there for the rest of his life. In 1485 he married Elisabeth Bürgis from Basel, the daughter of a cutler. Elisabeth bore him seven children. Keen for his eldest son Onophrius to become a humanist, he taught him Latin in the cradle and enrolled him in university at the age of seven.

He first attracted attention in humanistic circles by his Latin poetry, and edited many ecclesiastical and legal works; but he is now only known by his famous satire, *Das Narrenschiff*, published by Bergmann in 1494, the popularity and influence of which were not limited to Germany. Under the form of an allegory, a ship laden with fools and steered by fools goes to the fools' paradise of Narragonia. Brant here lashes with unsparing vigour the weaknesses and vices of his time. Here he conceives Saint Grobian, whom he imagines to be the patron saint of vulgar and coarse people.

Returning to Strasbourg in 1500, Brant made several petitions to the Emperor Maximilian to drive back the Turks in order to save the West. But when he realises that the Emperor is not up to the task, he writes to his fellow humanist Konrad Peutinger in Augsburg in 1504 that the role of Emperor could equally well be carried out by another people if the Germans were incapable of fulfilling the role that history had given them. In the same spirit, in 1492 he had sung the praises of Ferdinand II of Aragon, for having conquered the Moors and unified Spain. A staunch proponent of German cultural nationalism, he believed that moral reform was necessary for the security of the Empire against the threat of the Turkish hordes.

Although, like most of the German humanists, essentially conservative in his religious views, Brant's eyes were open to the abuses in the church, and the *Narrenschiff* was a most effective preparation for the Protestant Reformation. Alexander Barclay's *Ship of Fools* (1509) is a free imitation of the German poem, and a Latin version by Jacobus Locher (1497) was hardly less popular than the German original.

There is also a large quantity of other "fool literature." Nigel, called Wireker (fl. 1190), a monk of Christ Church Priory, Canterbury, wrote a satirical *Speculum stultorum*, in which the ambitious and discontented monk figured as the ass Brunellus, who wanted a longer tail. Brunellus, who was educated in Paris, decides to found an order of fools, which shall combine the good points of all the existing monastic orders. *Cock Lovell's Bate* (printed by Wynkyn de Worde, c. 1510) is another imitation of the *Narrenschiff*. Cock Lovell is a fraudulent currier who gathers round him a rascally collection of tradesmen. They sail off in a riotous fashion up hill and down dale throughout England. Brant's other works, of which the chief was a version of Freidank's *Bescheidenheit* (1508), are of inferior interest and importance.

Judeo-German

From the late 13th century, there is evidence of the beginnings of the Yiddish language, which in the early phase is a variety of Middle High German, not distinct enough even to be described as a dialect, but written in Hebrew characters. In its early phase, it is normally referred to as Judeo-German; from the 15th century it becomes Old Yiddish. Poems in this idiom belong equally to the fields of Medieval German Studies and Jewish/Yiddish studies.

Notable works include the 14th-century *Dukus Horant* (a narrative poem known as the "Jewish *Kudrun*") or the 15th-century *Bovo Bukh*, the most popular chivalric romance in the Yiddish language.

Dukus Horant

Dukus Horant is a 14th-century narrative poem in Judeo-German (Proto-Yiddish). It is the best known of a number of works which survive in the famous Cambridge Codex T.-S.10.K.22. This manuscript was discovered in the Cairo Geniza in 1896, and contains a collection of narrative poems in a variant of Middle High German, written in Hebrew characters. There is some controversy over the extent to which the manuscript's language differs from the commonly spoken German of the time, but it is agreed there is a strong Jewish colouring to it. Therefore these are the oldest known works (apart from a few short inscriptions dated to the 13th century) in the Ashkenazi Jewish vernacular which later developed into Yiddish.

Dukus Horant is a heroic epic with thematic similarities to the German poem *Kudrun*. It is thus a good example of the transfer of literary material between the Christian and Jewish communities in the German-speaking lands in the later Middle Ages. The other works in the manuscript contain traditional Jewish material.

Bovo Bukh

The *Bovo-Bukh* ("Bovo book"; also known as *Baba Buch*, etc.), written in 1507–1508 by Elia Levita, was the most popular chivalric romance in the Yiddish language. It was first printed in 1541, being the first non-religious book to be printed in Yiddish. For five centuries, it endured at least 40 editions. It is written in *ottava rima* and, according to Sol Liptzin, is "generally regarded as the most outstanding poetic work in Old Yiddish".

The theme derives from the Anglo-Norman romance of Sir Bevis of Hampton, by way of an Italian poem that had modified the name *Bevis of Hampton* to *Buovo d'Antona* and had, itself, been through at least thirty editions at the time of translation and adaptation into Yiddish. The central theme is the love of Bovo and Druziane [Gottheil] The story "had no basis in Jewish reality", but compared to other chivalric romances it "tone[s] down the Christian symbols of his original" and "substitute[s] Jewish customs, Jewish values and Jewish traits of character here and there..."

The character was also popular in Russian folk culture as Prince Bova. The *Bovo-Bukh* later became known in the late 18th century as the *Bove-mayse* or "Bovo's tale". This name, in turn, was corrupted and passed into the Yiddish language as *bubbe meise,* literally "grandmother's tale", meaning "old wives' tale".

Bovo's young mother conspires to have her husband, an aged king, killed during a hunt, then marries the murderer. They try and fail to poison the child Bovo, whom they are afraid will avenge his father. The handsome youth runs away from Antona, is kidnapped and taken to Flanders to be stable boy to a king, whose daughter Druzane falls in love with him.

The heathen sultan of Babylonia arrives, backed by ten thousand warriors, to demand Druzane in marriage for his ugly son, Lucifer. He is refused; in the ensuing war the king of Flanders is captured. Bovo, riding a magic horse Rundele, defeats the sultan's army, slays Lucifer, frees the king, and is promised the hand of Druzane, but is enticed to Babylonia, where he is horribly imprisoned for a year before escaping. Meanwhile, Druzane has presumed him dead and consented to marry the knight Macabron.

On the wedding day of Druzane and Macabron, Bovo arrives disguised as a beggar; he and Druzane flee, first to a palace but later to the forest, pursued by Macabron. Deep in the forest, Druzane gives birth to twins.

Bovo sets off to try to find a route back to Flanders. Druzane comes to the conclusion that Bovo has fallen prey to a lion, sets off on her own with the twins, and successfully reaches Flanders. Bovo returns to their forest abode; failing to find her or the twins, he now also presumes *her* to have fallen prey. Despairing, he joins an army ranged against his native Antona. He kills his stepfather, dispatches his mother to a nunnery, and takes his rightful crown. He is eventually reunited with Druzane, who becomes his queen.

Reformation (1500–1700)

The rise of the middle class in the 14th and 15th centuries and the struggles of the peasants against the nobility culminated in the great 16th-century religious revolution known as the Reformation. This movement was reflected in literature, especially by Martin Luther, whose translation of the Bible established New High German as the literary language of Germany. In secular literature the aristocratic *Minnesang* was discarded in favor of the *Meistergesang* ("master song"), written by guilds of artisans known as MEISTERSINGER. Also popular were the simple lyric poems later collectively titled *Volkslied*.

The *Schwank*, a farcical form of comic anecdote, gave popular expression to the stories of such sly rogues as Till Eulenspiegel. In the famous *Das Narrenschiff* (1494; *The Ship of Fools*, 1509) the humanist poet Sebastian Brant satirized more than 100 contemporary forms of foolishness and immorality. Another successful author was Johann Fischart (1546–90), a satiric poet and polemical writer for the Protestant cause, who based his material on the adventures of Gargantua and Pantagruel, characters created by the French satirist François Rabelais. This period marked the first appearance in literature of the legendary scholar Johann Faust in the anonymous prose fiction *Historia von Dr. Johann Fausten*, published in 1587.

Late in the 15th century German drama, hitherto restricted to passion plays and other religious spectacles, began to take on secular form in the *Fastnachtsspiele* ("Shrovetide plays"), allegorical comic dramas performed during the carnival season. Worldly elements gradually penetrated even the religious Christmas and Easter plays. Among the important dramatists of the Reformation period were Burkard Waldis (c. 1495–1557), who also wrote satiric fables, Nikodemus Frischlin (1547–90), and Hans Sachs, a poet and dramatist who was noted for his *Fastnachtsspiele.*

An attempt to bring French influences into German literature was made during the early 17th century by the critic Martin Opitz (1597–1639). In his principal work, *Das Buch von der deutschen Poeterey* (Book of German Poetry, 1624), Opitz demanded that German writers imitate contemporary French models in style, meter, and pattern. Although some of the literary academies carried his rules to extremes of complicated formality, several poets, influenced by Opitz, achieved an increased individuality of expression. Among them were Simon Dach (1605–59); Paul Flemming (1609–40); Johann Scheffler (1624–77), commonly called Angelus Silesius; and Baron Friedrich von Logau (1604–55). Protestant poetry of the 17th century reached its height in the hymns of Paul Gerhardt (1607–76).

The development of German literature was halted for more than a generation by the Thirty Years' War. The effects of the conflict can be seen in the work of the novelist Hans Jakob Christoph von Grimmelshausen. His tale of a disillusioned farmer's son, *Der abenteuerliche Simplicissimus* (1669; *The Adventurous Simplicissimus,* 1912), is the first great novel in the German language. Such comedies as *Peter Squenz* (1663) by the satirist Andreas Gryphius also describe the disillusionment and disenchantment that inevitably followed the war.

Medieval German Poetry

Minnesang

Minnesang was the tradition of lyric and song writing in Germany which flourished in the 12th century and continued into the 14th century. People who wrote and performed Minnesang are known as Minnesingers.

Minnesang has much in common with the troubadour tradition of France, and it likely stemmed from that tradition, though developed features unique to it. Like the troubadors, the Minnesingers mainly sang of courtly love (this is where the *Minne* part of their name comes from).

Several of the best known Minnesingers are also noted for their epic poetry, among them Wolfram von Eschenbach and Gottfried von Strassburg. Other noted Minnesingers include Dietmar von Aist, Neidhart von Reuental, Heinrich von Morungen, and Walther von der Vogelweide.

A number of Minnelied have survived to the present day, although mainly in manuscripts dating from the 15th century or later, which may present the songs in a form other than the original one. Additonally, it is often rather difficult to interpret the musical notation used to write them down. Although the contour of the melody can usually be made out, the rhythm of the song is frequently hard to fathom.

Minnesang died out in the 15th century, and the tradition of the Meistersingers began. The two traditions are quite different, however (Minnesingers were mainly aristocrats, while Meistersingers were merchants, for example).

At least two operas have been written about the Minnesang tradition: Richard Wagner's *Tannhuser* and Richard Strauss' *Guntram*.

Walther von der Vogelweide

Walther von der Vogelweide (c. 1170 - c. 1230) is the most celebrated of medieval German lyric poets. For all his fame, Walther's name is not found in contemporary records, with the exception of a solitary mention in the travelling accounts of Bishop Wolfger of Passau—"*Walthero cantori de Vogelweide pro pellicio V solidos longos*"—"To Walther the singer of the Vogelweide five shillings to buy a fur coat," and the main sources of information about him are his own poems and occasional references by contemporary Minnesingers. It is clear from the title *her* (*Herr*, Sir) these give him, that he was of noble birth; but it is equally clear from his name Vogelweide (Lat. *aviarium*, a gathering place or preserve of birds) that he belonged not to the higher nobility, who took their titles from castles or villages, but to the nobility of service (*Dienstadd*), humble retainers of the great lords, who in wealth and position were little removed from non-noble free cultivators.

For a long time the place of his birth was a matter of dispute, until Franz Pfeiffer established beyond reasonable doubt that he was born in the Wipthal in Tirol, where, not far from the little town of Sterzing on the Eisak, a wood—called the Vorder und Hintervogelweide—preserves at least the name of his vanished home. This origin would account for what is known of Walther's early life. Tirol was at this time the home of several noted *Minnesingers*; and the court of Vienna, under the enlightened duke Frederick I of the house of Babenberg, had become a centre of poetry and art.

Here it was that the young poet learned his craft under the renowned master Pemmar the Old, whose death he afterwards lamented in two of his most beautiful lyrics; and in the open handed duke he found his first patron. This happy period of his life, during which he produced the most charming and spontaneous of his love-lyrics, came to an end with the death of Duke Frederick in 1198. Henceforward Walther was a wanderer from court to court, singing for his lodging and his bread, and ever hoping that some patron would arise to save him from this "juggler's life" (*gougel-fuore*) and the shame of ever playing the guest. For material success in this profession he was hardly calculated. His criticism of men and manners was scathing; and even when this did not touch his princely patrons, their underlings often took measures to rid themselves of so uncomfortable a censor.

Thus he was forced to leave the court of the generous duke Bernhard of Carinthia (1202-1256); after an experience of the tumultuous household of the landgrave of Thuringia he warns those who have weak ears to give it a wide berth; and after three years at the court of Dietrich I of Meissen (reigned 1195-1221) he complains that he had received for his services neither money nor praise. Walther was, in fact, a man of strong views; and it is this which gives him his main significance in history, as distinguished from his place in literature. From the moment when the death of the emperor Henry VI (1197) opened the fateful struggle between empire and papacy, Walther threw himself ardently into the fray on the side of German independence and unity. Though his religious poems sufficiently prove the sincerity of his Catholicism, he remained to the end of his days opposed to the extreme claims of the popes, whom he attacks with a bitterness which can only be justified by the strength of his patriotic feelings. His political poems begin with an appeal to Germany, written in 1198 at Vienna, against the disruptive ambitions of the princes: "Crown Philip with the Kaiser's crown And bid them vex thy peace no more."

He was present, on September 8, at Philip's coronation at Mainz, and supported him till his victory was assured. After Philip's murder in 1209, he "said and sang" in support of Otto of Brunswick against the papal candidate Frederick of Staufen; and only when Otto's usefulness to Germany had been shattered by the battle of Bouvines (1212) did he turn to the rising star of Frederick II, now the sole representative of German majesty against pope and princes.

From the new emperor his genius and his zeal for the empire at last received recognition; and a small fief in Franconia was bestowed upon him, which, though he complained that its value was little, gave him the home and the fixed position he had so long desired. That Frederick gave him an even more signal mark of his favour by making him the tutor of his son Henry VII, is more than doubtful. The fact, in itself highly improbable, rests only upon the evidence of a single poem, which is capable of another interpretation. Walther's restless spirit did not suffer him to remain long on his new property.

In 1217 we find him once more at Vienna, and again in 1219 after the return of Duke Leopold VI from the crusade. About 1224 he seems to have settled on his fief near Wrzburg. He was active in urging the German princes to take part in the crusade of 1228, and may have accompanied the crusading army at least as far as his native Tirol. In a beautiful and pathetic poem he paints the change that had come over the scenes of his childhood and made his life seem a thing dreamed. He died about 1230, and was buried at Wrzburg, after leaving directions, according to the story, that the birds were to be fed at his tomb daily. The original gravestone with its Latin inscription has disappeared; but in 1843 a new monument was erected over the spot. There is also a fine statue of the poet at Bozen, unveiled in 1877.

Historically interesting as Walther's political verses are, their merit has been not a little exaggerated by modern German critics, who saw their own imperial aspirations and anti-papal prejudices reflected in this patriotic poet of the middle ages. Of more lasting value are the beautiful lyrics, mainly dealing with love, which led his contemporaries to hail him as their master in song (*unsers sanges meister*). He is of course unequal. At his worst he does not rise above the tiresome conventionalities of his school. At his best he shows a spontaneity, a charm and a facility which his rivals sought in vain to emulate. His earlier lyrics are full of the joy of life, of feeling for nature and of the glory of love. Greatly daring, he even rescues love from the convention which had made it the prerogative of the nobly born, contrasts the titles "woman" (*wip*) and "lady" (*frouwe*) to the disadvantage of the latter, and puts the most beautiful of his lyrics—*Unter der linden*—into the mouth of a simple girl. A certain seriousness, which is apparent under the joyousness of his earlier work, grew on him with years. Religious and didactic poems become more frequent; and his verses in praise of love turn at times to a protest against the laxer standards of an age demoralized by political unrest. Throughout his attitude is healthy and sane. He preaches the crusade; but at the same time he suggests the virtue of toleration, pointing out that in the worship of God, "Christians, Jews and heathen all agree."

He fulminates against "false love"; but pours scorn on those who maintain that "love is sin." In an age of monastic ideals and loose morality there was nothing commonplace in the simple lines in which he sums up the inspiring principle of chivalry at its best: "''Swer guotes wibes liebe hat Der schamt sich ieder missetat."

Altogether Walther's poems give us the picture not only of a great artistic genius, but of a strenuous, passionate, very human and very lovable character.

The *Gesichte* were edited by Karl Lachmann. This edition of the great scholar was re-edited by M. Haupt. *Walther v. d. Vogelweide,* edited by Franz Pfeiffer, with introduction and notes. *Glossarium zu d. Gedichten Walther's, nebste. Reimverzeichnis,* by CA Hornig. There are translations into modern German by B Obermann, and into English verse *Selected poems of Walter van der Vogelweide* by W Alison Phillips, with introduction and notes. The poem *Unter der Linden,* not included in the latter, was freely translated by TL Beddoe), more closely by WA Phillips in the *Nineteenth Century* for July 1896. *Leben u. Dichten Walther's van der Vogelweide,* by Wilhelm Wilmanns, is a valuable critical study of the poet's life and works.

Nibelungenlied

The *Nibelungenlied* is an epic poem in Middle High German taking Burgundian kings as its subject matter. It is the work of an anonymous 13th century poet from the Danube area. He re-worked various pagan heroic motifs into a work of courtly poetry.

The word Nibelungen has several meanings, referring to the Burgundian kings portrayed in the poem, and to the followers of Siegfried, and to a legendary race of Germanic dwarfs.

Sigurd proposes to Kriemhild, the beautiful sister of Gunther, Gernot and Giselher, three Burgundian kings. He is allowed to marry her after he defeats Brnhild, the queen of Iceland, with the aid of a cloak which lets him become invisible. Brnhild becomes Gunther's wife.

Kriemhild lets slip the secret in a row with Brnhild, and Hagen decides to kill Sigurd. He finds out his most vulnerable spot and kills him while they are hunting.

Attila the Hun now proposes to Kriemhild, and she invites the Burgundians to a feast in Hungary. There is a huge fight, and everyone is killed except Gunther and Hagen who are captured by Dietrich of Bern.

Kriemhild demands the return of the Nibelungen treasure (stolen by Hagen). When she fails to get it back, she arranges for Gunther to be killed and cuts off Hagen's head with Sigurd's sword. She in turn is killed by Hildebrand, Dietrich's armourer.

The *Niebelungenlied* served as source material for Wagner's "Ring Cycle" (*The Ring of the Nibelung* also known as *Der Ring des Nibelungen*).

5

Middle English Literature

The term Middle English literature refers to the literature written in the form of the English language known as Middle English, from the 12th century until the 1470s, when the Chancery Standard, a form of London-based English, became widespread and the printing press regularized the language.

Between the 1470s and the middle of the following century there is a transition to early Modern English though in literary terms the characteristics of the literary works written does not change radically until the effects of the Renaissance and Reformed Christianity become more apparent in the reign of King Henry VIII. There are three main categories of Middle English Literature: Religious, Courtly love, and Arthurian, though much of Chaucer's work stands outside these. Among the many religious works are those in the Katherine Group and the writings of Julian of Norwich and Richard Rolle.

Since the year 1169 and the Anglo-Norman "conquest," literature in Middle English started being written in Ireland. Its surviving quantity is comparatively small, but some is of premier historical and literary importance. It also exhibits an idiosyncratic combination of word spellings that permits us to identify it as medieval Hiberno-English, a distinctive written dialect of late Middle English.

One reason for the relative lack of surviving texts is the fact that from the late twelfth century to the fifteenth, English in Ireland was always a minority language, even if that of the powerful minority congregating in and around the colonial centers and the walled towns. (The other principal vernacular introduced after 1169, Anglo-Norman French, seems by the late fourteenth century to have been in substantial decline.)

Language

Middle English is the name given by historical linguists to the diverse forms of the English language in use between the late 11th century and about 1470, when the Chancery Standard, a form of London-based English, began to become widespread, a process aided by the introduction of the printing press into England by William Caxton in the late 1470s. By that time the variant of the Northumbrian dialect (prevalent in Northern England) spoken in southeast Scotland was developing into the Scots language. The language of England as used after this time, up to 1650, is known as Early Modern English.

Unlike Old English, which tended largely to adopt Late West Saxon scribal conventions in the immediate pre-Conquest period, Middle English as a written language displays a wide variety of scribal (and presumably dialectal) forms. However, the diversity of forms in written Middle English may signify neither greater variety of spoken forms of English than could be found in pre-Conquest England, nor a faithful representation of contemporary spoken English (though presumably greater fidelity to this than may be found in Old English texts).

Rather, this diversity suggests the gradual end of the role of Wessex as a focal point and trend-setter for scribal activity, and the emergence of more distinct local scribal styles and written dialects, and a general pattern of transition of activity over the centuries that follow, as Northumbria, East Anglia and London emerge successively as major centres of literary production, with their own generic interests.

Literary Background

The Norman conquest of England in 1066 traditionally signifies the beginning of 200 years of the domination of French in English letters. French cultural dominance, moreover, was general in Europe at this time. French language and culture replaced English in polite court society and had lasting effects on English culture.

But the native tradition survived, although little 13th-century, and even less 12th-century, vernacular literature is extant, since most of it was transmitted orally. Anglo-Saxon fragmented into several dialects and gradually evolved into Middle English, which, despite an admixture of French, is unquestionably English. By the mid-14th cent., Middle English had become the literary as well as the spoken language of England.

The poetry of some major Middle English authors was imported, including William Langland's *Piers Plowman* and Geoffrey Chaucer's *Troilus and Criaseyde* (the latter appears in a 1526 catalogue of the library of the earl of Kildare). Some ambitious Middle English prose translations were also undertaken by Irishmen, including in 1422 one done by James Yonge of Dublin of the French *Secreta Secretorum.* At about this time an anonymous translator also rendered into English the late twelfth-century Latin *Expugnatio Hibernica* of Giraldus Cambrensis.

However, the most important Middle English literary collection to have survived is contained in London, Harley MS 913, an anthology mainly of verse on religious and satirical topics, compiled probably by a Franciscan friar in Waterford circa 1331. Some of his items were imported, but many are indigenous, one of the most striking being *The Land of Cokaygne,* a surreal account of monastic hedonism in which abbeys are built of food, and geese fly ready-cooked into the open mouth.

Outside the Harley anthology, Middle English poetry from Ireland is not otherwise extensive. Middle English lyrics are known from Kilkenny and from Armagh, for example, but their quantity is small. Absence of evidence is not evidence of absence, however. The field of drama is similar, where the chance survival of part of the text of *The Pride of Life,* the earliest known morality play in English, suggests that a dramatic tradition formerly existed that was far broader and sturdier than this solitary, sophisticated play might otherwise lead us to suspect.

Early Period

After the Norman conquest of England, the written form of the Anglo-Saxon language continued in some monasteries but few literary works are known from this period. The new aristocracy spoke French, and this became the standard language of courts, parliament, and polite society. As the invaders integrated, their language and literature mingled with that of the natives: the Norman French dialect of the upper classes became Anglo-Norman, and Anglo-Saxon underwent a gradual transition into Middle English. Since the political power was no longer in English hands the West Saxon literary language had no more influence than any other dialect so Middle English literature is written in many dialects depending on the situation of the writers.

While Anglo-Norman or Latin was preferred for high culture and administration, English literature by no means died out, and a number of important works illustrate the development of the language. Around the turn of the thirteenth century, Layamon wrote his *Brut*, based on Wace's twelfth century Anglo-Norman epic of the same name; Layamon's language is recognisably Middle English, though his prosody shows a strong Anglo-Saxon influence remaining.

Other transitional works were preserved as popular entertainment, including a variety of romances and lyrics. With time, the English language regained prestige, and in 1362 it replaced French and Latin in Parliament and courts of law. Early examples of Middle English literature are the Ormulum and Havelock the Dane.

The Mercian dialect thrived between the 8th and 13th centuries and was referred to by John Trevisa, writing in 1387:

> *For men of the est with men of the west, as it were undir the same partie of hevene, acordeth more in sownynge of speche than men of the north with men of the south, therfore it is that Mercii, that beeth men of myddel Engelond, as it were parteners of the endes, understondeth better the side langages, northerne and southerne, than northerne and southerne understondeth either other...*

The Thirteenth Century

Middle English prose of the 13th cent. continued in the tradition of Anglo-Saxon prose—homiletic, didactic, and directed toward ordinary people rather than polite society. The "Katherine Group", comprising three saints' lives, is typical. The Ancren Riwle is a manual for prospective anchoresses; it was very popular, and it greatly influenced the prose of the 13th and 14th cent. The fact that there was no French prose tradition was very important to the preservation of the English prose tradition.

In the 13th cent. the romance, an important continental narrative verse form, was introduced in England. It drew from three rich sources of character and adventure: the legends of Charlemagne, the legends of ancient Greece and Rome, and the British legends of King Arthur and the Knights of the Round Table. Layamon's Brut, a late 13th-century metrical romance (a translation from the French), marks the first appearance of Arthurian matter in English. Original English romances based upon indigenous material include King Horn and Havelok the Dane, both 13th-century works that retain elements of the Anglo-Saxon heroic tradition.

However, French romances, notably the Arthurian romances of Chrétien de Troyes, were far more influential than their English counterparts. In England French romances popularized ideas of adventure and heroism quite contrary to those of Anglo-Saxon heroic literature and were representative of wholly different values and tastes. Ideals of courtly love, together with its elaborate manners and rituals, replaced those of the heroic code; adventure and feats of courage were pursued for the sake of the knight's lady rather than for the sake of the hero's honor or the glory of his tribal king.

Continental verse forms based on metrics and rhyme replaced the Anglo-Saxon alliterative line in Middle English poetry (with the important exception of the 14th-century alliterative revival). Many French literary forms also became popular, among them the fabliau; the exemplum, or moral tale; the animal fable; and the dream vision. The continental allegorical tradition, which derived from classical literature, is exemplified by the Roman de la Rose, which had a strong impact on English literature.

Medieval works of literature often center on a popular rhetorical figure, such as the *ubi sunt,* which remarks on the inevitability—and sadness—of change, loss, and death; and the *cursor mundi,* which harps on the vanity of human grandeur. A 15,000-line 13th-century English poem, the *Cursor Mundi,* retells human history (i.e., the medieval version—biblical plus classical story) from the point of view its title implies.

A number of 13th-century secular and religious Middle English lyrics are extant, including the exuberant Sumer Is Icumen In, but like Middle English literature in general, the lyric reached its fullest flower during the second half of the 14th cent. Lyrics continued popular in the 15th cent., from which time the ballad also dates.

Fourteenth Century

The poetry of the alliterative revival, the unexplained reemergence of the Anglo-Saxon verse form in the 14th cent., includes some of the best poetry in Middle English. The Christian allegory *The Pearl* is a poem of great intricacy and sensibility that is meaningful on several symbolic levels. *Sir Gawain and the Green Knight,* by the same anonymous author, is also of high literary sophistication, and its intelligence, vividness, and symbolic interest render it possibly the finest Arthurian poem in English. Other important alliterative poems are the moral allegory *Piers Plowman,* attributed to William Langland, and the alliterative *Morte Arthur,* which, like nearly all English poetry until the mid-14th cent., was anonymous.

The works of Geoffrey Chaucer mark the brilliant culmination of Middle English literature. Chaucer's *The Canterbury Tales* are stories told each other by pilgrims—who comprise a very colorful cross section of 14th-century English society—on their way to the shrine at Canterbury.

The tales are cast into many different verse forms and genres and collectively explore virtually every significant medieval theme. Chaucer's wise and humane work also illuminates the full scope of medieval thought. Overshadowed by Chaucer but of some note are the works of John Gower.

Fifteenth Century

The 15th cent. is not distinguished in English letters, due in part to the social dislocation caused by the prolonged Wars of the Roses. Of the many 15th-century imitators of Chaucer the best-known are John Lydgate and Thomas Hoccleve. Other poets of the time include Stephen Hawes and Alexander Barclay and the Scots poets William Dunbar, Robert Henryson, and Gawin Douglas. The poetry of John Skelton, which is mostly satiric, combines medieval and Renaissance elements.

William Caxton introduced printing to England in 1475 and in 1485 printed Sir Thomas Malory's *Morte d'Arthur.* This prose work, written in the twilight of chivalry, casts the Arthurian tales into coherent form and views them with an awareness that they represent a vanishing way of life. The miracle play, a long cycle of short plays based upon biblical episodes, was popular throughout the Middle Ages in England. The morality play, an allegorical drama centering on the struggle for man's soul, originated in the 15th cent. The finest of the genre is Everyman.

Late Period

It was with the fourteenth century that major works of English literature began once again to appear; these include the so-called Pearl Poet's *Pearl, Patience, Cleanness,* and *Sir Gawain and the Green Knight;* Langland's political and religious allegory *Piers Plowman;* Gower's *Confessio Amantis;* and, of course, the works of Chaucer, the most highly regarded English poet of the Middle Ages, who was seen by his contemporaries as a successor to the great tradition of Virgil and Dante.

The latter portion of the 14th century also saw not only the consolidation of English as a written language, taking over from French or Latin in certain areas, but a large shift from primarily theological or religious subject matter to that of a more secular nature. Literature during this period also saw a growth in the amount of (secular) books being copied in English. Thus, the latter portion of the 14th century can be seen as the most significant period in the history of the English language.

The reputation of Chaucer's successors in the 15th century has suffered in comparison with him, though Lydgate and Skelton are widely studied. However, the century really belongs to a group of remarkable Scottish writers. The rise of Scottish poetry began with the writing of *The Kingis Quair* by James I of Scotland. The main poets of this Scottish group were Robert Henryson, William Dunbar and Gavin Douglas. Henryson and Douglas introduced a note of almost savage satire, which may have owed something to the Gaelic bards, while Douglas's version of Virgil's *Aeneid* is one of the early monuments of Renaissance literary humanism in English.

Many morality plays and miracle plays were produced. Sidrak and Bokkus is an example of late Middle English literature.

Caxton and the English Language

William Caxton printed four-fifths of his works in English. He translated a large number of works into English; Caxton translated 26 of the titles himself. Caxton is credited with printing as many as 108 books, 87 of which were different titles. However, the English language was changing rapidly in Caxton's time and the works he was given to print were in a variety of styles and dialects. Caxton was a technician rather than a writer and he often faced dilemmas concerning language standardisation in the books he printed. (He wrote about this subject in the preface to his *Eneydos*) His successor Wynkyn de Worde faced similar problems.

Caxton is credited with standardising the English language (that is, homogenising regional dialects) through printing. This facilitated the expansion of

English vocabulary, the development of inflection and syntax and the ever-widening gap between the spoken and the written word. However, Richard Pynson, a Frenchman who started printing in London in 1491 or 1492 and who favoured Chancery Standard, was a more accomplished stylist and consequently pushed the English language further toward standardisation.

Several poems in early Middle English are extant. The Orrmulum, a verse translation of parts of the Gospels, is of linguistic and prosodic rather than literary interest. Of approximately the same date, *The Owl and the Nightingale* is the first example in English of the *débat,* a popular continental form; in the poem, the owl, strictly monastic and didactic, and the nightingale, a free and amorous secular spirit, charmingly debate the virtues of their respective ways of life.

Role of King Arthur in Literature

King Arthur is a legendary British leader who, according to medieval histories and romances, led the defence of Britain against the Saxon invaders in the early 6th century. The details of Arthur's story are mainly composed of folklore and literary invention, and his historical existence is debated and disputed by modern historians. The sparse historical background of Arthur is gleaned from various sources, including the *Annales Cambriae,* the *Historia Brittonum,* and the writings of Gildas. Arthur's name also occurs in early poetic sources such as *Y Gododdin.*

The legendary Arthur developed as a figure of international interest largely through the popularity of Geoffrey of Monmouth's fanciful and imaginative 12th-century *Historia Regum Britanniae (History of the Kings of*

Britain). However, some Welsh and Breton tales and poems relating the story of Arthur date from earlier than this work; in these works, Arthur appears either as a great warrior defending Britain from human and supernatural enemies or as a magical figure of folklore, sometimes associated with the Welsh Otherworld, Annwn. How much of Geoffrey's *Historia* (completed in 1138) was adapted from such earlier sources, rather than invented by Geoffrey himself, is unknown.

Although the themes, events and characters of the Arthurian legend varied widely from text to text, and there is no one canonical version, Geoffrey's version of events often served as the starting point for later stories. Geoffrey depicted Arthur as a king of Britain who defeated the Saxons and established an empire over Britain, Ireland, Iceland, Norway and Gaul. In fact, many elements and incidents that are now an integral part of the Arthurian story appear in Geoffrey's *Historia*, including Arthur's father Uther Pendragon, the wizard Merlin, the sword Excalibur, Arthur's birth at Tintagel, his final battle against Mordred at Camlann and final rest in Avalon.

The 12th-century French writer Chrétien de Troyes, who added Lancelot and the Holy Grail to the story, began the genre of Arthurian romance that became a significant strand of medieval literature. In these French stories, the narrative focus often shifts from King Arthur himself to other characters, such as various Knights of the Round Table. Arthurian literature thrived during the Middle Ages but waned in the centuries that followed until it experienced a major resurgence in the 19th century. In the 21st century, the legend lives on, not only in literature but also in adaptations for theatre, film, television, comics and other media.The historical basis for the King Arthur legend has long been debated by scholars. One school of thought, citing entries in the *Historia Brittonum* (*History of the Britons*) and *Annales Cambriae* (*Welsh Annals*), sees Arthur as a genuine historical figure, a Romano-British leader who fought against the invading Anglo-Saxons sometime in the late 5th to early 6th century. The *Historia Brittonum*, a 9th-century Latin historical compilation attributed in some late manuscripts to a Welsh cleric called Nennius, lists twelve battles that Arthur fought. These culminate in the Battle of Mons Badonicus, or Mount Badon, where he is said to have single-handedly killed 960 men. Recent studies, however, question the reliability of the *Historia Brittonum* as a source for the history of this period.

The other text that seems to support the case for Arthur's historical existence is the 10th-century *Annales Cambriae*, which also link Arthur with the Battle of Mount Badon. The *Annales* date this battle to 516–518, and also mention the Battle of Camlann, in which Arthur and Medraut (Mordred) were both killed, dated to 537–539. These details have often been used to bolster confidence in the *Historia*'s account and to confirm that Arthur really did fight at Mount Badon. Problems have been identified, however, with using this source to support the *Historia Brittonum*'s account. The latest research shows that the *Annales Cambriae* was based on a chronicle begun in the late 8th century in Wales.

Additionally, the complex textual history of the *Annales Cambriae* precludes any certainty that the Arthurian annals were added to it even that early. They were more likely added at some point in the 10th century and may never have existed in any earlier set of annals. The Mount Badon entry probably derived from the *Historia Brittonum.*

This lack of convincing early evidence is the reason many recent historians exclude Arthur from their accounts of post-Roman Britain. In the view of historian Thomas Charles-Edwards, "at this stage of the enquiry, one can only say that there may well have been an historical Arthur [but ...] the historian can as yet say nothing of value about him". These modern admissions of ignorance are a relatively recent trend; earlier generations of historians were less sceptical. Historian John Morris made the putative reign of Arthur the organising principle of his history of sub-Roman Britain and Ireland, *The Age of Arthur* (1973). Even so, he found little to say about a historical Arthur.

Partly in reaction to such theories, another school of thought emerged which argued that Arthur had no historical existence at all. Morris's *Age of Arthur* prompted archaeologist Nowell Myres to observe that "no figure on the borderline of history and mythology has wasted more of the historian's time". Gildas' 6th-century polemic *De Excidio et Conquestu Britanniae* (*On the Ruin and Conquest of Britain*), written within living memory of Mount Badon, mentions the battle but does not mention Arthur.

Arthur is not mentioned in the *Anglo-Saxon Chronicle* or named in any surviving manuscript written between 400 and 820. Arthur is absent from Bede's early 8th-century *Ecclesiastical History of the English People,* another major early source for post-Roman history that mentions Mount Badon. Historian David Dumville has written that he thought we could dispose him [Arthur] quite briefly. David owes his place in history books to a 'no smoke without fire' school of thought... The fact of the matter is that there is no historical evidence about Arthur; he must be rejected from histories and, above all, from the titles of books.

Some scholars argue that Arthur was originally a fictional hero of folklore – or even a half-forgotten Celtic deity – who became credited with real deeds in the distant past. They cite parallels with figures such as the Kentish totemic horse-gods Hengest and Horsa, who later became historicised. Bede ascribed to these legendary figures a historical role in the 5th-century Anglo-Saxon conquest of eastern Britain. It is not even certain that Arthur was considered a king in the early texts.

Historical documents for the post-Roman period are scarce, so a definitive answer to the question of Arthur's historical existence is unlikely. Sites and places have been identified as "Arthurian" since the 12th century, but archaeology can confidently reveal names only through inscriptions found in secure contexts. The so-called "Arthur stone", discovered in 1998 among the ruins at Tintagel Castle in Cornwall in securely dated 6th-century contexts, created a brief stir but proved irrelevant. Other inscriptional evidence for Arthur, including the Glastonbury cross, is tainted with the suggestion of forgery. Although several historical figures have been proposed as the basis for Arthur, no convincing evidence for these identifications has emerged.

Medieval Literary Traditions

The creator of the familiar literary persona of Arthur

was Geoffrey of Monmouth, with his pseudo-historical *Historia Regum Britanniae* (*History of the Kings of Britain*), written in the 1130s. The textual sources for Arthur are usually divided into those written before Geoffrey's *Historia* (known as pre-Galfridian texts, from the Latin form of Geoffrey, *Galfridus*) and those written afterwards, which could not avoid his influence (Galfridian, or post-Galfridian, texts).

Pre-Galfridian Traditions

The earliest literary references to Arthur come from Welsh and Breton sources. There have been few attempts to define the nature and character of Arthur in the pre-Galfridian tradition as a whole, rather than in a single text or text/story-type. One recent academic survey that does attempt this, by Thomas Green, identifies three key strands to the portrayal of Arthur in this earliest material.

The first is that he was a peerless warrior who functioned as the monster-hunting protector of Britain from all internal and external threats. Some of these are human threats, such as the Saxons he fights in the *Historia Brittonum*, but the majority are supernatural, including giant cat-monsters, destructive divine boars, dragons, dogheads, giants and witches. The second is that the pre-Galfridian Arthur was a figure of folklore (particularly topographic or onomastic folklore) and localised magical wonder-tales, the leader of a band of superhuman heroes who live in the wilds of the landscape. The third and final strand is that the early Welsh Arthur had a close connection with the Welsh Otherworld, Annwn.

On the one hand, he launches assaults on Otherworldly fortresses in search of treasure and frees their prisoners. On the other, his warband in the earliest sources includes former pagan gods, and his wife and his possessions are clearly Otherworldly in origin.

One of the most famous Welsh poetic references to Arthur comes in the collection of heroic death-songs known as *Y Gododdin* (*The Gododdin*), attributed to the 6th-century poet Aneirin. In one stanza, the bravery of a warrior who slew 300 enemies is praised, but it is then noted that despite this "he was no Arthur", that is to say his feats cannot compare to the valour of Arthur. *Y Gododdin* is known only from a 13th-century manuscript, so it is impossible to determine whether this passage is original or a later interpolation, but John Koch's view that the passage dates from a 7th-century or earlier version is regarded as unproven; 9th- or 10th-century dates are often proposed for it. Several poems attributed to Taliesin, a poet said to have lived in the 6th century, also refer to Arthur, although these all probably date from between the 8th and 12th centuries. They include "Kadeir Teyrnon" ("The Chair of the Prince"), which refers to "Arthur the Blessed", "Preiddeu Annwn" ("The Spoils of Annwn"), which recounts an expedition of Arthur to the Otherworld, and "Marwnat vthyr pen[dragon]" ("The Elegy of Uther Pen[dragon]"), which refers to Arthur's valour and is suggestive of a father-son relationship for Arthur and Uther that pre-dates Geoffrey of Monmouth.

Other early Welsh Arthurian texts include a poem found in the *Black Book of Carmarthen*, "Pa gur yv y porthaur?" ("What man is the gatekeeper?"). This takes the form of a dialogue between Arthur and the gatekeeper of a fortress he wishes to enter, in which Arthur recounts the names and deeds of himself and his men, notably Cei (Kay) and Bedwyr (Bedivere). The Welsh prose tale *Culhwch and Olwen* (c. 1100), included in the modern Mabinogion collection, has a much longer list of more than 200 of Arthur's men, though Cei and Bedwyr again take a central place. The story as a whole tells of Arthur helping his kinsman Culhwch win the hand of Olwen, daughter of Ysbaddaden Chief-Giant, by completing a series of apparently impossible tasks, including the hunt for the great semi-divine boar Twrch Trwyth.

The 9th-century *Historia Brittonum* also refers to this tale, with the boar there named Troy(n)t. Finally, Arthur is mentioned numerous times in the *Welsh Triads,* a collection of short summaries of Welsh tradition and legend which are classified into groups of three linked characters or episodes in order to assist recall.

The later manuscripts of the Triads are partly derivative from Geoffrey of Monmouth and later continental traditions, but the earliest ones show no such influence and are usually agreed to refer to pre-existing Welsh traditions. Even in these, however, Arthur's court has started to embody legendary Britain as a whole, with "Arthur's Court" sometimes substituted for "The Island of Britain" in the formula "Three XXX of the Island of Britain".While it is not clear from the *Historia Brittonum* and the *Annales Cambriae* that Arthur was even considered a king, by the time *Culhwch and Olwen* and the Triads were written he had become *Penteyrnedd yr Ynys hon,* "Chief of the Lords of this Island", the overlord of Wales, Cornwall and the North.

In addition to these pre-Galfridian Welsh poems and tales, Arthur appears in some other early Latin texts besides the *Historia Brittonum* and the *Annales Cambriae*. In particular, Arthur features in a number of well-known *vitae* ("Lives") of post-Roman saints, none of which are now generally considered to be reliable historical sources (the earliest probably dates from the 11th century). According to the *Life of Saint Gildas*, written in the early 12th century by Caradoc of Llancarfan, Arthur is said to have killed Gildas' brother Hueil and to have rescued his wife Gwenhwyfar from Glastonbury.

In the *Life of Saint Cadoc*, written around 1100 or a little before by Lifris of Llancarfan, the saint gives protection to a man who killed three of Arthur's soldiers, and Arthur demands a herd of cattle as *wergeld* for his men. Cadoc delivers them as demanded, but when Arthur takes possession of the animals, they turn into bundles of ferns. Similar incidents are described in the medieval biographies of Carannog, Padarn and Eufflam, probably written around the 12th century.

A less obviously legendary account of Arthur appears in the *Legenda Sancti Goeznovii*, which is often claimed to date from the early 11th century although the earliest manuscript of this text dates from the 15th century. Also important are the references to Arthur in William of Malmesbury's *De Gestis Regum Anglorum* and Herman's *De Miraculis Sanctae Mariae Laudensis*, which together provide the first certain evidence for a belief that Arthur was not actually dead and would at some point return, a theme that is often revisited in post-Galfridian folklore.

Geoffrey of Monmouth

The first narrative account of Arthur's life is found in

Geoffrey of Monmouth's Latin work *Historia Regum Britanniae* (*History of the Kings of Britain*). This work, completed c. 1138, is an imaginative and fanciful account of British kings from the legendary Trojan exile Brutus to the 7th-century Welsh king Cadwallader.

Geoffrey places Arthur in the same post-Roman period as do *Historia Brittonum* and *Annales Cambriae.* Arthur incorporates Arthur's father, Uther Pendragon, his magician advisor Merlin, and the story of Arthur's conception, in which Uther, disguised as his enemy Gorlois by Merlin's magic, sleeps with Gorlois's wife Igerna at Tintagel, and she conceives Arthur. On Uther's death, the fifteen-year-old Arthur succeeds him as King of Britain and fights a series of battles, similar to those in the *Historia Brittonum,* culminating in the Battle of Bath.

Arthur then defeats the Picts and Scots before creating an Arthurian empire through his conquests of Ireland, Iceland and the Orkney Islands. After twelve years of peace, Arthur sets out to expand his empire once more, taking control of Norway, Denmark and Gaul. Gaul is still held by the Roman Empire when it is conquered, and Arthur's victory naturally leads to a further confrontation between his empire and Rome's. Arthur and his warriors, including Kaius (Kay), Beduerus (Bedivere) and Gualguanus (Gawain), defeat the Roman emperor Lucius Tiberius in Gaul but, as he prepares to march on Rome, Arthur hears that his nephew Modredus (Mordred) – whom he had left in charge of Britain – has married his wife Guenhuuara (Guinevere) and seized the throne.

Arthur returns to Britain and defeats and kills Modredus on the river Camblam in Cornwall, but he is mortally wounded. Arthur hands the crown to his kinsman Constantine and is taken to the isle of Avalon to be healed of his wounds, never to be seen again.

How much of this narrative was Geoffrey's own invention is open to debate. Certainly, Geoffrey seems to have made use of the list of Arthur's twelve battles against the Saxons found in the 9th-century *Historia Brittonum,* along with the battle of Camlann from the *Annales Cambriae* and the idea that Arthur was still alive. Arthur's personal status as the king of all Britain would also seem to be borrowed from pre-Galfridian tradition, being found in *Culhwch and Olwen,* the *Triads* and the Saints' Lives.

Finally, Geoffrey borrowed many of the names for Arthur's possessions, close family and companions from the pre-Galfridian Welsh tradition, including Kaius (Cei), Beduerus (Bedwyr), Guenhuuara (Gwenhwyfar), Uther (Uthyr) and perhaps also Caliburnus (Caledfwlch), the latter becoming Excalibur in subsequent Arthurian tales. However, while names, key events and titles may have been borrowed, Brynley Roberts has argued that "the Arthurian section is Geoffrey's literary creation and it owes nothing to prior narrative."

So, for instance, the Welsh Medraut is made the villainous Modredus by Geoffrey, but there is no trace of such a negative character for this figure in Welsh sources until the 16th century. There have been relatively few modern attempts to challenge this notion that the *Historia Regum Britanniae* is primarily Geoffrey's own work, with scholarly opinion often echoing William of Newburgh's late-12th-century comment that Geoffrey "made up" his narrative, perhaps through an "inordinate love of lying".

Geoffrey As he is one dissenter from this view, believing that Geoffrey's narrative is partially derived from a lost source telling of the deeds of a 5th-century British king named Riotamus, this figure being the original Arthur, although historians and Celticists have been reluctant to follow Ashe in his conclusions.

Whatever his sources may have been, the immense popularity of Geoffrey's *Historia Regum Britanniae* cannot be denied. Well over 200 manuscript copies of Geoffrey's Latin work are known to have survived, and this does not include translations into other languages. Thus, for example, around 60 manuscripts are extant containing Welsh-language versions of the *Historia*, the earliest of which were created in the 13th century; the old notion that some of these Welsh versions actually underlie Geoffrey's *Historia*, advanced by antiquarians such as the 18th-century Lewis Morris, has long since been discounted in academic circles.

As a result of this popularity, Geoffrey's *Historia Regum Britanniae* was enormously influential on the later medieval development of the Arthurian legend. While it was by no means the only creative force behind Arthurian romance, many of its elements were borrowed and developed (e.g., Merlin and the final fate of Arthur), and it provided the historical framework into which the romancers' tales of magical and wonderful adventures were inserted.

The popularity of Geoffrey's Historia and its other derivative works (such as Wace's Roman de Brut) is generally agreed to be an important factor in explaining the appearance of significant numbers of new Arthurian works in continental Europe during the 12th and 13th centuries, particularly in France. It was not, however, the only Arthurian influence on the developing "Matter of Britain". There is clear evidence for a knowledge of Arthur and Arthurian tales on the Continent before Geoffrey's work became widely known, as well as for the use of "Celtic" names and stories not found in Geoffrey's Historia in the Arthurian romances. From the perspective of Arthur, perhaps the most significant effect of this great outpouring of new Arthurian story was on the role of the king himself: much of this 12th-century and later Arthurian literature centres less on Arthur himself than on characters such as Lancelot and Guenevere, Perceval, Galahad, Gawain, and Tristan and Isolde. Whereas Arthur is very much at the centre of the pre-Galfridian material and Geoffrey's Historia itself, in the romances he is rapidly sidelined. His character also alters significantly.

In both the earliest materials and Geoffrey he is a great and ferocious warrior, who laughs as he personally slaughters witches and giants and takes a leading role in all military campaigns, whereas in the continental romances he becomes the roi fainéant, the "do-nothing king", whose "inactivity and acquiescence constituted a central flaw in his otherwise ideal society". Arthur's role in these works is frequently that of a wise, dignified, even-tempered, somewhat bland, and occasionally feeble monarch.

So, he simply turns pale and silent when he learns of Lancelot's affair with Guinevere in the Mort Artu, whilst in Chrétien de Troyes's Yvain, the Knight of the Lion he is unable to stay awake after a feast and has to retire for a nap. Nonetheless, as Norris J. Lacy has observed, whatever his faults and frailties may be in these Arthurian romances, "his prestige is never – or almost never – compromised by his personal weaknesses... his authority and glory remain intact."

Arthur and his retinue appear in some of the *Lais* of Marie de France, but it was the work of another French poet, Chrétien de Troyes, that had the greatest influence with regard to the above development of the character of Arthur and his legend. Chrétien wrote five Arthurian romances between c. 1170 and c. 1190.

Erec and Enide and *Cligès* are tales of courtly love with Arthur's court as their backdrop, demonstrating the shift away from the heroic world of the Welsh and Galfridian Arthur, while *Yvain, the Knight of the Lion* features Yvain and Gawain in a supernatural adventure, with Arthur very much on the sidelines and weakened. However, the most significant for the development of the Arthurian legend are *Lancelot, the Knight of the Cart,* which introduces Lancelot and his adulterous relationship with Arthur's queen (Guinevere), extending and popularising the recurring theme of Arthur as a cuckold, and *Perceval, the Story of the Grail,* which introduces the Holy Grail and the Fisher King and which again sees Arthur having a much reduced role.

Chrétien was thus "instrumental both in the elaboration of the Arthurian legend and in the establishment of the ideal form for the diffusion of that legend", and much of what came after him in terms of the portrayal of Arthur and his world built upon the foundations he had laid. *Perceval,* although unfinished, was particularly popular: four separate continuations of the poem appeared over the next half century, with the notion of the Grail and its quest being developed by other writers such as Robert de Boron, a fact that helped accelerate the decline of Arthur in continental romance. Similarly, Lancelot and his cuckolding of Arthur with Guinevere became one of the classic motifs of the Arthurian legend, although the Lancelot of the prose *Lancelot* and later texts was a combination of Chrétien's character and that of Ulrich von Zatzikhoven's *Lanzelet*. Chrétien's work even appears to feed back into Welsh Arthurian literature, with the result that the romance Arthur began to replace the heroic, active Arthur in Welsh literary tradition. Particularly significant in this development were the three Welsh Arthurian romances, which are closely similar to those of Chrétien, albeit with some significant differences: *Owain, or the Lady of the Fountain* is related to Chrétien's *Yvain*; *Geraint and Enid*, to *Erec and Enide*; and *Peredur son of Efrawg*, to *Perceval*.

Up to c. 1210, continental Arthurian romance was expressed primarily through poetry; after this date the tales began to be told in prose. The most significant of these 13th-century prose romances was the Vulgate Cycle (also known as the Lancelot-Grail Cycle), a series of five Middle French prose works written in the first half of that century. These works were the *Estoire del Saint Grail*, the *Estoire de Merlin*, the *Lancelot propre* (or Prose *Lancelot*, which made up half the entire Vulgate Cycle on its own), the *Queste del Saint Graal* and the *Mort Artu*, which combine to form the first coherent version of the entire Arthurian legend.

The cycle continued the trend towards reducing the role played by Arthur in his own legend, partly through the introduction of the character of Galahad and an expansion of the role of Merlin. It also made Mordred the result of an incestuous relationship between Arthur and his sister and established the role of Camelot, first mentioned in passing in Chrétien's

Lancelot, as Arthur's primary court. This series of texts was quickly followed by the Post-Vulgate Cycle (c. 1230–40), of which the *Suite du Merlin* is a part, which greatly reduced the importance of Lancelot's affair with Guinevere but continued to sideline Arthur, now in order to focus more on the Grail quest. As such, Arthur became even more of a relatively minor character in these French prose romances; in the Vulgate itself he only figures significantly in the *Estoire de Merlin* and the *Mort Artu*.

The development of the medieval Arthurian cycle and the character of the "Arthur of romance" culminated in *Le Morte d'Arthur*, Thomas Malory's retelling of the entire legend in a single work in English in the late 15th century. Malory based his book – originally titled *The Whole Book of King Arthur and of His Noble Knights of the Round Table* – on the various previous romance versions, in particular the Vulgate Cycle, and appears to have aimed at creating a comprehensive and authoritative collection of Arthurian stories. Perhaps as a result of this, and the fact that *Le Morte D'Arthur* was one of the earliest printed books in England, published by William Caxton in 1485, most later Arthurian works are derivative of Malory's.

Post-medieval Literature

The end of the Middle Ages brought with it a waning of interest in King Arthur. Although Malory's English version of the great French romances was popular, there were increasing attacks upon the truthfulness of the historical framework of the Arthurian romances – established since Geoffrey of Monmouth's time – and thus the legitimacy of the whole Matter of Britain. So, for example, the 16th-century humanist scholar Polydore Vergil famously rejected the claim that Arthur was the ruler of a post-Roman empire, found throughout the post-Galfridian medieval "chronicle tradition", to the horror of Welsh and English antiquarians. Social changes associated with the end of the medieval period and the Renaissance also conspired to rob the character of Arthur and his associated legend of some of their power to enthral audiences, with the result that 1634 saw the last printing of Malory's *Le Morte d'Arthur* for nearly 200 years. King Arthur and the Arthurian legend were not entirely abandoned, but until the early 19th century the material was taken less seriously and was often used simply as vehicle for allegories of 17th- and 18th-century politics.

Thus Richard Blackmore's epics *Prince Arthur* (1695) and *King Arthur* (1697) feature Arthur as an allegory for the struggles of William III against James II. Similarly, the most popular Arthurian tale throughout this period seems to have been that of Tom Thumb, which was told first through chapbooks and later through the political plays of Henry Fielding; although the action is clearly set in Arthurian Britain, the treatment is humorous and Arthur appears as a primarily comedic version of his romance character.

Tennyson and The Revival

In the early 19th century, medievalism, Romanticism, and the Gothic Revival reawakened interest in Arthur and the medieval romances. A new code of ethics for 19th-century gentlemen was shaped around the chivalric ideals that the "Arthur of romance" embodied. This renewed interest first made itself felt in 1816, when Malory's *Le Morte d'Arthur* was reprinted for the first time since 1634. Initially the medieval Arthurian legends were of particular interest to poets, inspiring, for example, William Wordsworth to write "The Egyptian Maid" (1835), an allegory of the Holy Grail. Pre-eminent among these was Alfred Lord Tennyson, whose first Arthurian poem, "The Lady of Shalott", was published in 1832.

Although Arthur himself played a minor role in some of these works, following in the medieval romance tradition, Tennyson's Arthurian work reached its peak of popularity with *Idylls of the King,* which reworked the entire narrative of Arthur's life for the Victorian era. First published in 1859, it sold 10,000 copies within the first week. In the *Idylls,* Arthur became a symbol of ideal manhood whose attempt to establish a perfect kingdom on earth fails, finally, through human weakness. Tennyson's works prompted a large number of imitators, generated considerable public interest in the legends of Arthur and the character himself, and brought Malory's tales to a wider audience. Indeed, the first modernisation of Malory's great compilation of Arthur's tales was published shortly after *Idylls* appeared, in 1862, and there were six further editions and five competitors before the century ended.

This interest in the "Arthur of romance" and his associated stories continued through the 19th century and into the 20th, and influenced poets such as William Morris and Pre-Raphaelite artists including Edward Burne-Jones. Even the humorous tale of Tom Thumb, which had been the primary manifestation of Arthur's legend in the 18th century, was rewritten after the publication of *Idylls.* While Tom maintained his small stature and remained a figure of comic relief, his story now included more elements from the medieval Arthurian romances, and Arthur is treated more seriously and historically in these new versions. The revived Arthurian romance also proved influential in the United States, with such books as Sidney Lanier's *The Boy's King Arthur* (1880) reaching wide audiences and providing inspiration for Mark Twain's satiric *A Connecticut Yankee in King Arthur's Court* (1889).

Although the "Arthur of romance" was sometimes central to these new Arthurian works (as he was in Burne-Jones's *The Last Sleep of Arthur in Avalon*, 1881–1898), on other occasions he reverted back to his medieval status and is either marginalised or even missing entirely, with Wagner's Arthurian operas providing a notable instance of the latter. Furthermore, the revival of interest in Arthur and the Arthurian tales did not continue unabated. By the end of the 19th century, it was confined mainly to Pre-Raphaelite imitators, and it could not avoid being affected by the First World War, which damaged the reputation of chivalry and thus interest in its medieval manifestations and Arthur as chivalric role model. The romance tradition did, however, remain sufficiently powerful to persuade Thomas Hardy, Laurence Binyon and John Masefield to compose Arthurian plays, and T. S. Eliot alludes to the Arthur myth (but not Arthur) in his poem *The Waste Land*, which mentions the Fisher King.

Modern Legend

In the latter half of the 20th century, the influence of the romance tradition of Arthur continued, through novels such as T.H. White's *The Once and Future King* (1958) and Marion Zimmer Bradley's *The Mists of Avalon* (1982) in addition to comic strips such as *Prince Valiant* (from 1937 onward). Tennyson had reworked the romance tales of Arthur to suit and comment upon the issues of his day, and the same is often the case with modern treatments too. Bradley's tale, for example, takes a feminist approach to Arthur and his legend, in contrast to the narratives of Arthur found in medieval materials, and American authors often rework the story of Arthur to be more consistent with values such as equality and democracy. The romance Arthur has become popular in film and theatre as well. T. H. White's novel was adapted into the Lerner-Loewe stage musical *Camelot* (1960) and the Disney animated film *The Sword in the Stone* (1963); *Camelot* itself, with its focus on the love of Lancelot and Guinevere and the cuckolding of Arthur, was itself made into a film of the same name in 1967. The romance tradition of Arthur is particularly evident and, according to critics, successfully handled in Robert Bresson's *Lancelot du Lac* (1974), Eric Rohmer's *Perceval le Gallois* (1978) and perhaps John Boorman's fantasy film *Excalibur* (1981); it is also the main source of the material utilised in the Arthurian spoof *Monty Python and the Holy Grail* (1975).

Re-tellings and re-imaginings of the romance tradition are not the only important aspect of the modern legend of King Arthur. Attempts to portray Arthur as a genuine historical figure of c. 500 AD, stripping away the "romance", have also emerged. As Taylor and Brewer have noted, this return to the medieval "chronicle tradition"' of Geoffrey of Monmouth and the *Historia Brittonum* is a recent trend which became dominant in Arthurian literature in the years following the outbreak of the Second World War, when Arthur's legendary resistance to Germanic invaders struck a chord in Britain. Clemence Dane's series of radio plays, *The Saviours* (1942), used a historical Arthur to embody the spirit of heroic resistance against desperate odds, and Robert Sherriff's play *The Long Sunset* (1955) saw Arthur rallying Romano-British resistance against the Germanic invaders. This trend towards placing Arthur in a historical setting is also apparent in historical and fantasy novels published during this period. In recent years the portrayal of Arthur as a real hero of the 5th century has also made its way into film versions of the Arthurian legend, most notably *King Arthur* (2004) and *The Last Legion* (2007).

Arthur has also been used as a model for modern-day behaviour. In the 1930s, the Order of the Fellowship of the Knights of the Round Table formed in Britain to promote Christian ideals and Arthurian notions of medieval chivalry. In the United States, hundreds of thousands of boys and girls joined Arthurian youth groups, such as the Knights of King Arthur, in which Arthur and his legends were promoted as wholesome exemplars. However, Arthur's diffus [illegible] ontemporary culture goes beyond such obviously Arthurian endeavours, with Arthurian names being regularly attached to objects, buildings and places.

As Norris J. Lacy has observed, "The popular notion of Arthur appears to be limited, not surprisingly, to a few motifs and names, but there can be no doubt of the extent to which a legend born many centuries ago is profoundly embedded in modern culture at every level.

6

Mediaeval Welsh Literature

The Welsh language evolved sometime between AD 400 and 700; the earliest surviving literature in Welsh is poetry dating from this period. The poetic tradition represented in the work of *Y Cynfeirdd* ("The Early Poets"), as they are known, then survives for over a thousand years to the work of the *Poets of the Nobility* in the 16th century.

The core tradition was praise poetry and the poet Taliesin was regarded as the first in the line. The other aspect of the tradition was the professionalism of the poets and their reliance on patronage from kings, princes and nobles in their turn for their living. The fall of the Kingdom of Gwynedd and the loss of any form of Welsh independence in 1282 proved a crisis in the tradition, but one that was eventually overcome. It led to the innovation the development of the cywydd meter, a more loose definition of praise, and a reliance on the nobility for patronage.

The professionalism of the poetic tradition was sustained by a Guild of Poets, or Order of Bards, with its own "rule book" emphasising the making of poetry as a craft. Under its rules poets undertook an apprenticeship of nine years to become fully qualified.

The rules also set out the payment a poet could expect for his work. These payments varied according to how long a poet had been in training and also the demand for poetry at particular times during the year.

Alongside the court poet, kings, princes and nobles patronised an official storyteller (Welsh: *cyfarwydd*). Like poets, the storytellers were also professionals; but, unlike the poets, little of their work has survived. What has survived are literary creations based on native Welsh tales which would have been told by the storytellers. The bulk of this material is found in the collection known today as the *Mabinogion*. Medieval Welsh prose was not confined to the story tradition, but also included a large body of both religious and practical works, in addition to a large amount translated from other languages.

Welsh Poetry before 1100

In Welsh literature the period before 1100 is known as the period of *Y Cynfeirdd* ("The earliest poets") or *Yr Hengerdd* ("The old poetry"). It roughly dates from the birth of the Welsh language until the arrival of the Normans in Wales towards the end of the 11th century.

The oldest Welsh literature does not belong to the territory know as Wales today, but rather to northern England and southern Scotland, and would have been composed in Cumbric, a Brythonic dialect closely related to Old Welsh. But though it is dated to the 6th, 7th, and 8th centuries, it has survived only in and 13th and 14th century manuscript copies. Some of these early poets' names are known from the 8th century *Historia Brittonum*, traditionally ascribed to the historian Nennius. The *Historia* lists the famous poets from the time of King Ida, AD 547-559:

> "At that time, Talhaiarn Tataguen was famed for poetry, and Neirin [Aneirin], and Taliesin, and Bluchbard, and Cian, who is called Guenith Guaut, were all famous at the same time in British [that is Brythonic, or, Welsh] poetry."

Of the poets named here it is believed that work that can be identified as Aneirin's and Taliesin's have survived.

Taliesin

The poetry of Taliesin has been preserved in a 14th century manuscript known as Llyfr Taliesin (Book of Taliesin). This manuscript contains a large body of later mystical poetry attributed to the poet, but scholars have recognised twelve poems that belong to the 6th century. They are all poems of praise: one for Cynan Garwyn, king of Powys about 580; two for Gwallawg, king of Elmet, a kingdom based around the modern Leeds; the other nine poems are associated with Urien Rheged, a ruler of the kingdom of Rheged, located around the Solway Firth, and with his son, Owain.

Taliesin's verse in praise of Urien and Owain became models for later poets, who turned to him for inspiration as they praised their own patrons in terms that he had used for his.

Aneirin

Aneirin, a near-contemporary of Taliesin, wrote a series of poems to create one long epic called *Y Gododdin*. It records the Battle of Catraeth, fought between the Britons of the kingdom of Gododdin (centred on Eidyn, the modern Edinburgh) and the Saxon kingdoms of Deira and Bernicia in the northeast of England. This battle was fought at Catterick in about the year 598. It has survived in Llyfr Aneirin (The Book of Aneirin), a manuscript dating from ca. 1265.

Llywarch Hen and Heledd

The poetry associated with Llywarch Hen (Llywarch the Elder) and Heledd date from a somewhat later period. These poems, in the form of monologues, express the sorrow and affliction felt at the loss of eastern portion of the Kingdom of Powys (present-day Shropshire) to the English. But they are also works where nature is an important element in the background, reflecting the main action and feelings of the poetry itself.

Other Early Poetry

Though the Anglo-Saxon invaders seem to break Welsh hearts in most of the early poetry, there are some poems of encouragement and the hope of an eventual and decisive defeat that would drive them back into the sea. One such poem is the tenth-century Armes Prydein from the Book of Taliesin which sees a coalition of Celtic and Scandinavian forces defeating the English and restoring Britain to the Welsh.

This period also produced religious poetry, such as the englynion in praise of the Trinity found in the ninth-century Juvencus Manuscript (Cambridge MS Ff. 4.42), which is now at Cambridge University Library. In the Book of Taliesin, 9th century poem *Edmyg Dinbych* (*In Praise of Tenby,* a town in Pembrokeshire), probably produced by a court poet in Dyfed to celebrate the New Year (Welsh: *Calan*). The book also includes important poems which were probably not composed by Taliesin, including the *Armes Prydein* (*The Great Prophecy of Britain*) and *Preiddeu Annwfn*, (*The Spoils of Annwn*), and the Book of Aneirin has preserved an early Welsh nursery rhyme, *Pais Dinogad* (*Dinogad's Petticoat*). Much of the nature poetry, gnomic poetry, prophetic poetry, and religious poetry in the Black Book of Carmarthen and the Red Book of Hergest is also believed to date from this period.

Welsh Poetry 1100-1600

From ca. 1100 to 1600 Welsh poetry can be divided roughly into two distinct periods: the period of the *Poets of the Princes* who worked before the loss of Welsh independence in 1282 and the *Poets of the Nobility* who worked from 1282 until the period of the English incorporation of Wales in the sixteenth century.

Poets of the Princes (ca. 1100-ca. 1300)

In Welsh this period is known as *Beirdd y Tywysogion* (Poets of the Princes) or *Y Gogynfeirdd* (The Less Early Poets). The main source for the poetry of the twelfth and thirteenth centuries is the Hendregadredd manuscript, an anthology of court poetry brought together at the Cistercian Strata Florida Abbey from about 1282 until 1350.

The poets of this period were professionals who worked in the various princely courts in Wales. They were members of a Guild of poets whose rights and responsibilities were enshrined in native Welsh law; and as such, they worked within a developed literary culture and with inflexible traditions. Bardic families were still common — the poet Meilyr Brydydd had a poet son and at least two poet grandsons — but it was becoming more and more usual for the craft of poetry to be taught formally, in bardic schools which might only be run by the *pencerdd* (chief musician). The *pencerdd* was the top of his profession and a special chair was set aside for him in the court, in an honoured position next to the heir. When he performed he was expected to sing twice: once in honour of God, and once in honour of the king. The *bardd teulu* (retinue poet) was one of the 24 officers of the court and he was responsible for singing for the military retinue before going into battle, and for the queen in the privacy of her chamber. The lowest ranking poets were the *cerddorion* (musicians).

The poetry praises the military prowess of the prince in a language that is deliberately antiquarian and obscure, echoing the earlier praise poetry tradition of Taliesin. There is also some religious poems and poetry in praise of women. With the death of the last native prince of Wales in 1282 the tradition gradually disappears. In fact, Gruffudd ab yr Ynad Coch's elegy on the death of Llywelyn ap Gruffudd, is one of the most notable poems of the era. Other prominent poets of this period include:

1) Meilyr Brydydd
2) Bleddyn Fardd
3) Cynddelw Brydydd Mawr
4) Dafydd Benfras
5) Llywarch ap Llywelyn

A rather different poet of this period was Hywel ab Owain Gwynedd who as the son of Prince Owain Gwynedd, was not a professional poet.

Poets of the Nobility

The poetic tradition thrived in Wales as long as there were patrons available to welcome its practitioners. The fact that, until 1282, Wales consisted of a number of 'kingdoms', each with its own independent ruler, ensured that there was no shortage of courts available to the travelling professional poet or "bard". After 1282 the poetic tradition survived by turning to the land-owning nobility to act as patrons, and these included some Norman lords who had successfully integrated themselves with the Welsh.

Much of the poetry of this period is praise poetry praise of the patron and his family, his ancestors, his house and his generosity and the cywydd is the most popular poetic meter used. Because of the popularity of the cywydd this period is also known as the period of the *Cywyddwyr* (poets who write using the cywydd meter). The poetry was very often sung to the accompaniment of the harp.

Though praise was the main matter of poetry, satire also thrived. The poets organised themselves into a Guild to protect their professional status, and from time to time their rules were revised and updated. Perhaps the most important being the decisions concerning patronage and poetic rank made at the Caerwys eisteddfod of 1523. The work of numerous poets of this period survives, some are anonymous, but very many are identified. Here are a few of the most prominent and influential are listed.

Dafydd ap Gwilym

Wales's greatest poet worked during the period of the Poets of the Nobility. For more information about his life and work.

Iolo Goch

From the Vale of Clwyd, Iolo Goch bridged between the period of the Poets of the Princes and Poets of the Nobility. Early in his career he composed in the tradition of the Poets of the Princes but he was among the first to sing the praises of the nobles and others using the cywydd meter. His main patron was Ithel ap Robert from Coedymynydd near Caerwys. Perhaps his most famous work is a cywydd poem in praise of Owain Glynduar's home at Sycharth.

Sion Cent

Traditionally associated with Breconshire, Siôn Cent is most famous for using his poetry in the service of his Christian beliefs and standing outside the tradition of praise of patron. Siôn Cent uses the cywydd meter for his work but in order to attack the sins of this world. Perhaps his most famous poem is *I wagedd ac oferedd y byd* (=In praise of the vanity and wantoness of the world). Siôn Cent turns his back on the praise of nobles which is as flattery and falsehood and sets his eyes on the blessedness of heaven.

Guto'r Glyn

Guto'r Glyn is associated with Glyn Ceiriog, Denbighshire, where many of his patrons lived. Glyn also wrote poems for other patrons in the four corners of Wales whose houses he visited on his journeys. Glyn was a master of the praise tradition in poetry. Guto was also a soldier who fought on the Yorkist side during the War of the Roses, but spent his last years as a lay guest at the Cistercian abbey of Valle Crucis, near Llangollen.

Dafydd Nanmor

Dafydd Nanmor, born at Nanmor (or Nantmor), Gwynedd, is one of the most significant poets of this period. It is said that he was exiled to south Wales for over-stepping the mark in his poetry and spent the rest of his life outside Gwynedd. His work was seen to have particular significance by the twentieth-century critic Saunders Lewis. Lewis saw him a poet of philosophy who praised the ideal ruler as he praised his patrons who saw that within the Welsh tradition all who had privilege and power also had responsibilities towards family, community and nation.

Other Voices in Poetry 1300 – 1600

Not all of the poetry which survives from this period belongs to the tradition of the praise poetry of the nobility. Some groups of poets and genres of poetry stood completely outside that tradition. Women seem to be totally excluded from the Welsh poetic guild, or Order of bards. It is known that some women did master the Welsh poetic craft and wrote poetry at this time, but only the work of one woman has survived in significant numbers, that of Gwerful Mechain.

The prophetic poetry was a means of reacting to and commenting upon political situations and happenings. This poetry is intentionally ambiguous and difficult to understand. But at its heart it prophesies victory for the Welsh over their enemies, the English. This poetry looked towards a man of destiny who would free them from their oppressors. With the victory of the 'Welshman' Henry VII in 1485 at the battle of Bosworth the poets believed that the prophecies had been fulfilled and the tradition comes to an end. Satire poetry was part of the 'official' poets' repertoire and sparingly used within the praise tradition to chastise a miserly patron. But it was in private poetic bouts with fellow poets that the satire tradition flourished.

Welsh Prose

It is believed that the earliest written Welsh is a marginal note of some sixty-four words in *Llyfr Teilo* (*The Book of St. Teilo*), a gospel book originating in Llandeilo but now in the library of St. Chad's Cathedral, Lichfield, and also known as the *Lichfield Gospels*, or, *The Book of St. Chad*. The marginal note, known from its opening (Latin) word as *The Surexit memorandum*, dates from the ninth century, or even earlier, and is a record of a legal case over land.

The native Welsh storyteller, known as the *cyfarwydd* ("the one who knows") was an official of the court. He was expected to know the traditional knowledge and the tales. But the storytelling tradition was basically oral, and only a few remnants suggest the wealth of that tradition. Amongst the most important are *Trioedd Ynys Prydain*, or the Welsh Triads, a compendium of mnemonics for poets and storytellers. The stories that have survived are literary compositions based on oral tradition.

In the Middle Ages Welsh was used for all sorts of purposes and this is reflected in the type of prose materials that has survived from this period: original material and translations, tales and facts, religious and legal, history and medicine.

Native Welsh Tales

The name *Mabinogion* is a convenient label for a collection of tales preserved in two manuscripts known as the White book of Rhydderch and the Red Book of Hergest. They are written in Middle Welsh, the common literary language between the end of the eleventh century and the fourteenth century. They include the four tales that form *Pedair Cainc y Mabinogi* ("The Four Branches of the Mabinogi"):

1) Pwyll prince of Dyfed;
2) Branwen daughter of Llwar;
3) Manawydan son of Llwar;
4) Math son of Mathonwy.

Two are native tales embodying traditions about King Arthur:

1) *Culhwch and Olwen* the earliest Arthurian tale in any language;
2) *The Dream of Rhonabwy*.

Two more are native tales embodying traditions about the early history of Britain:

1) *Lludd and Llefelys;*
2) *The Dream of Maxen.*

The final three are the Arthurian Welsh Romances, showing the influence of French poet Chrétien de Troyes:

1) *Owain, or the Lady of the Fountain,* from *Yvain, the Knight of the Lion;*
2) *Geraint and Enid,* from *Erec and Enide;*
3) *Peredur son of Efrog,* from *Perceval, the Story of the Grail.*

Welsh Legal Texts

Tradition holds that Hywel Dda summoned a conference at Whitland, Carmarthenshire, in about 945.

At this conference Welsh law was codified and set down in writing for posterity. Since the earliest manuscripts containing these legal texts date from about two hundred and fifty years after the event they are probably not a record of what was codified there, if such a conference was even convened. In fact, until the annexation of Wales in 1536, native Welsh law grew and developed organically and for that reason many more copies of it have survived than of the native tales.

The use of Welsh for legal texts shows that it had the words and the technical terms with definite and exact meanings needed in such circumstances. It also shows that reading and writing Welsh was not confined to priests and monks, but that there were also lawyers "whose skill is directed not to administrating the law (there were judges for that), but to writing it, to giving it permanence in words, to ordering words and sentences in such a way that what was stated should be quite clear".

Religious Texts

The vast majority of Welsh religious texts from the Middle Ages are translations and mostly the works of unknown monks and priests. The works themselves reflect the tastes and fashions of Christendom at the time: apocryphal narratives, dreams or visions, theological treatises and exegesis, and mystical wLives of the saints

About thirty lives of the saints, both native ones like Beuno, Curig, and Gwenfrewi and the more general such as the Mary, the mother of Jesus, Mary Magdalene, Martin of Tours, and Catherine of Alexandria survive, all translations into Welsh from

Latin. Even the lives of the native saints were composed in Latin originally, and that a long time after the saint's actual life and so of little or no interest to those looking for actual historical information. Perhaps the two most important is *Buchedd Dewi* ("The life of Dewi, or, David") written by Rhygyfarch in about 1094, and *Buchedd Cadog* (*Life of Cadog") written by Lifris of Llancarfan in ca. 1100.*

History Texts

The Welsh medieval history texts belong to the class of literary creations, but the split into two distinct groups. While the first group, *Brut y Tywysogion*, tends to stick to historical facts, the second, *Brut y Brenhinedd*, is the fantastic creation of Geoffrey of Monmouth.

Brut y Tywysogion

Brut y Tywysogion (*Chronicle of the Princes*) are variant Welsh translation of a Latin original *annales* telling the history of Wales from the seventh century to the death of Llywelyn ap Gruffudd in 1282. It is believed that original and its translation were produced at the Cistercian Strata Florida Abbey.

Brut y Brenhinedd

Brut y Brenhinedd (*Chronicle of the Kings*) is the name given to a number of texts that ultimately trace their origins back to translations of Geoffrey of Monmouth's Historia Regum Britanniae (1136). As such they were key works in shaping how the Welsh thought of themselves and others, tracing their origins back to Brutus, the mythical founder of the Britain. In fact the Welsh word *brut* is derived from Brutus's name and originally meant "a history of Brutus" and then "a chronicle history".

7

Anglo-Norman Literature

Anglo-Norman literature, body of literature written in England, in the French dialect known as Anglo-Norman, from c.1100 to c.1250. Initiated at the court of Henry I, it was supported by the wealthy, French-speaking aristocracy who controlled England after the Norman conquest. The dominant literary forms were histories, sacred and secular biographies, and homilies; romance and fiction were relatively scarce. Perhaps the most important historian was Geoffrey Gaimer, whose two-part history of England, *Histoire des Bretons* and *Estorie des Engles,* was written in verse. Philippe of Thaün, the earliest known Anglo-Norman poet, was noted for the moral allegory the *Bestiaire.* Of secular works, Thomas's *Tristan* is notable both artistically and as an early source for the Tristram and Isolde legend.

Background

The Norman language came over to England with William the Conqueror. Following the Norman conquest, the Norman language became the language of England's nobility. During the whole of the 12th century Anglo-Norman (the variety of Norman used in England) shared with Latin the distinction of being the literary language of England, and it was in use at the court until the 14th century. It was not until the reign of Henry VII that English became the native tongue of the kings of England. After the loss of the French provinces, schools for the teaching of French were established in England, among the most celebrated of which we may quote that of Marlborough. The language had undergone certain changes which distinguished it from the Old Norman spoken in Normandy; but, except for some graphical characteristics, from which certain rules of pronunciation are to be inferred, the changes to which the language was subjected were the individual modifications of the various authors, so that, while we may still speak of Anglo-Norman writers, an Anglo-Norman language, properly so called, gradually ceased to exist.

It was not till 1363 that the chancellor opened the parliamentary session with an English speech, and not until the reign of Henry VII that Statute law ceased to be written in Anglo-Norman. And although the Hundred Years' War led to a decline in the study of French and the disappearance of Anglo-Norman literature, the French language continued, through some vicissitudes, to be the classical language of the courts of justice until the 17th century. French, alongside Latin, remained the language of government until the mid-1480s. It is still an official language in the Channel Islands (*Jersey Legal French*), though English has become dominant since 1901.

The most flourishing period of Anglo-Norman literature was from the beginning of the 12th century to the end of the first quarter of the 13th. The end of this period is generally said to coincide with the loss of the French provinces to Philip Augustus, but literary and political history do not correspond quite so precisely, and the end of the first period would be more accurately denoted by the appearance of the history of William the Marshal in 1225.

Wace and Benoît de Sainte-More compiled their histories at his bidding, and it was in his reign that Marie de France composed her poems. An event with which he was closely connected, viz. the murder of Thomas Becket, gave rise to a whole series of writings, some of which are purely Anglo-Norman.

In his time appeared the works of Béroul and Thomas of Britain respectively, as well as some of the most celebrated of the Anglo-Norman *romans d'aventure*. It is important to keep this fact in mind when studying the different works which Anglo-Norman literature. These works will be examined briefly, grouping them into narrative, didactic, hagiographic, lyric, satiric and dramatic literature.

Epic and Romance

The French epic came over to England at an early date. It is believed that the *Chanson de Roland* was sung at the battle of Hastings, and some Anglo-Norman manuscripts of chansons de geste have survived to this day. The *Pélérinage de Charlemagne* was, for instance, only preserved in an Anglo-Norman manuscript of the British Museum (now lost), although the author was certainly a Parisian. The oldest manuscript of the *Chanson de Roland* that is also a manuscript written in England, and amongst the others of less importance may mention *La Chançun de Willame,* the MS. of which has been published in facsimile at Chiswick.

Although the diffusion of epic poetry in England did not actually inspire any new *chansons de geste,* it developed the taste for this class of literature, and the epic style in which the tales of the *Romance of Horn,* of *Bovon de Hampton,* of *Guy of Warwick,* of *Waldef,* and of *Fulk Fitz Warine* are treated, is certainly partly due to this circumstance. Although the last of these works has come down to us only in a prose version, it contains unmistakable signs of a previous poetic form, and what possess is really only a rendering into prose similar to the transformations undergone by many of the *chansons de geste.*

The interinfluence of French and English literature can be studied in the Breton romances and the *romans d'aventure* even better than in the epic poetry of the period. The *Lay of Orpheus* is known to us only through an English imitation, *Sir Orfeo;* the *Lai du cor* was composed by Robert Biket, an Anglo-Norman poet of the 12th century. The *The Lais of Marie de France* were written in England, and the greater number of the romances composing the *matière de Bretagne* seem to have passed from England to France through the medium of Anglo-Norman.

The legends of Merlin and Arthur, collected in the *Historia Regum Britanniae* by Geoffrey of Monmouth, passed into French literature, bearing the character which the bishop of St Asaph had stamped upon them. Chrétien de Troyes's *Perceval* is doubtless based on an Anglo-Norman poem. Robert de Boron took the subject of his Merlin from Geoffrey of Monmouth.

Finally, the most celebrated love-legend of the Middle Ages, and one of the most beautiful inventions of world-literature, the story of Tristan and Iseult, tempted two authors, Béroul and Thomas, the first of whom is probably, and the second certainly, Anglo-Norman. One *Folie Tristan* was composed in England in the last years of the 12th century.

Less fascinating than the story of Tristan and Iseult, but nevertheless of considerable interest, are the two *romans d'aventure* of Hugh of Rutland, *Ipomedon* and *Protesilaus* written about 1185. The first relates the adventures of a knight who married the young duchess of Calabria, niece of King Meleager of Sicily, but was loved by Medea, the king's wife.

The second poem is the sequel to *Ipomedon,* and deals with the wars and subsequent reconciliation between Ipomedon's sons, Daunus, the elder, lord of Apulia, and Protesilaus, the younger, lord of Calabria. Protesilaus defeats Daunus, who had expelled him from Calabria. Daunus saves his brother's life, is reinvested with the dukedom of Calabria, and, after the death of Daunus, succeeds to Apulia. Daunus subsequently marries Medea, King Meleager's widow, who had helped him to seize Apulia, having transferred her affection for Ipomedon to his younger son.

To these two romances by an Anglo-Norman author, *Amadas et Idoine,* of which only a continental version is possessed, is to be added. Gaston Paris has proved indeed that the original was composed in England in the 12th century.

The Anglo-Norman poem on the *Life of Richard Coeur de Lion* is lost, and an English version only has been preserved. About 1250 Eustace of Kent introduced into England the *roman d'Alexandre* in his *Roman de toute chevalerie,* many passages of which have been imitated in one of the oldest English poems on Alexander, namely, *King Alisaunder.*

Fableaux, Fables and Religious Tales

In spite of the incontestable popularity enjoyed by this class of literature, only some half-dozen *fableaux* have been written in England, viz.

1) Le chevalier a la corbeille,
2) Le chevalier qui faisait parler les muets,
3) Le chevalier, sa dame et un clerc,
4) Les trois dames,
5) La gageure,
6) Le pretre d'Alison,
7) La bourgeoise d'Orléans.

As to fables, one of the most popular collections in the Middle Ages was that written by Marie de France, which she claimed to have translated from King Alfred. In the *Contes moralisés,* written by Nicole Bozon shortly before 1320, a few fables bear a strong resemblance to those of Marie de France.

The religious tales deal mostly with the Mary Legends, and have been handed down to us in three collections:

1. The Adgar's collection. Most of these were translated from William of Malmesbury by Adgar in the 12th century.
2. The collection of Everard of Gateley, a monk of St. Edmund at Bury, who wrote *c.* 1250 three Mary Legends.
3. An anonymous collection of sixty Mary Legends composed, some of which have been published in Hermann Suchier's *Bibliotheca Normannica;* in the *Altf. Bibl.*

Another set of religious and moralising tales is to be found in Chardri's *Set dormans* and *Josaphat, c.* 1216.

Anglo-Norman Historiography

Of far greater importance, however, are the works which constitute Anglo-Norman historiography. The first Anglo-Norman historiographer is Geoffrey Gaimar, who wrote his *Estorie des Angles* for Dame Constance, wife of Ralph FitzGilbert. This history comprised a first part (now lost), which was merely a translation of Geoffrey of Monmouth's *Historia Regum Britanniae,* preceded by a history of the Trojan War, and a second part which carries us as far as the death of William Rufus. For this second part he has consulted historical documents, but he stops at the year 1087, just when he has reached the period about which he might have been able to give us some first-hand information.

The *History of the Dukes of Normandy* by Benoît de Sainte-More is based on the work of Wace. It was composed at the request of Henry II. about 1170, and takes us as far as the year 1135. The 43,000 lines which it contains are of but little interest to the historian; they are too evidently the work of a *romancier courtois,* who takes pleasure in recounting love-adventures such as those he has described in his romance of Troy. Other works, however, give us more trustworthy information, for example, the anonymous poem on Henry II.'s *Conquest of Ireland* in 1172, which, together with the *Expugnatio hibernica* of Giraud de Barri, constitutes our chief authority on this subject. The *Conquest of Ireland* was republished in 1892 by Goddard Henry Orpen, under the title of *The Song of Dermot and the Earl.* Similarly, Jourdain Fantosme, who was in the north of England in 1174, wrote an account of the wars between Henry II., his sons, William the Lion of Scotland and Louis VII., in 1173 and 1174. Not one of these histories, however, is to be compared in value with *The History of William the Marshal, Count of Striguil and Pembroke,* regent of England from 1216–1219, which was found and subsequently edited by Paul Meyer.

This masterpiece of historiography was composed in 1225 or 1226 by a professional poet of talent at the request of William, son of the marshal. It was compiled from the notes of the marshal's squire, John d'Early, who shared all the vicissitudes of his master's life and was one of the executors of his will. This work is of great value for the history of the period 1186–1219, as the information furnished by John d'Early is either personal or obtained at first hand.

In the part which deals with the period before 1186, it is true, there are various mistakes, due to the ignorance of contemporary history, but these slight blemishes are amply atoned for by the literary value of the work. The style is concise, the anecdotes are well told, the descriptions short and picturesque; the whole constitutes one of the most living pictures of medieval society.

Very pale by the side of this work appear the *Chronique* of Peter of Langtoft, written between 1311 and 1320, and mainly of interest for the period 1294-1307; the *Chronique* of Nicholas Trevet, dedicated to Princess Mary, daughter of Edward I. which carries us to the year 1362-1363; the *Black Prince,* a poem by the poet Chandos Herald, composed about 1386, and relating the life of the Black Prince from 1346-1376; and, lastly, the different versions of the *Brutes,* the form and historical importance of which have been indicated by Paul Meyer, and by F.W.D. Brie.

Finally as ancient history mention the translation of Eutropius and Dares, by Geoffrey of Waterford (13th century), who gave also the *Secret des Secrets,* a translation from a work wrongly attributed to Aristotle, which belongs to the next division.

Didactic Literature

Didactic literature is the most considerable, if not the most interesting, branch of Anglo-Norman literature: it comprises a large number of works written chiefly with the object of giving both religious and profane instruction to Anglo-Norman lords and ladies. The following list gives the most important productions arranged in chronological order:

1) Philippe de Thaun, *Comput,* c. 1119, poem on the calendar;
2) *Bestiaire,* c. 1130;
3) *Lois de Guillaume le Conquérant;*
4) *Oxford Psalter,* c. 1150;
5) *Cambridge Psalter,* c. 1160;
6) *London Psalter,* same as Oxford Psalter;
7) *Disticha Catonis,* translated by Everard de Kirkham and Elie de Winchester;
8) *Le Roman de fortune,* a summary of Boethius' *De consolatione philosophiae* (*Consolation of Philosophy*), by Simon de Fresne;
9) *Quatre livres des rois,* translated into French in the 12th century, and imitated in England soon after;

10) *Donnei des Amanz,* the conversation of two lovers, overheard and carefully noted by the poet, of a purely didactic character, in which are included three interesting pieces, the first being an episode of the story of Tristram, the second a fable, *L'homme et le serpent,* the third a tale, *L'homme et l'oiseau,* which is the basis of the celebrated *Lai de l'oiselet;*
11) *Livre des Sibiles;*
12) *Enseignements Trebor,* by Robert de Ho;
13) *Lapidaire de Cambridge;*
14) Frére Angier de Ste. Frideswide, *Dialogues,* 29th of November 1212;
15) *Li dialoge Grégoire le pape,* ed. by Foerster, 1876; *Petit Plet,* by Chardri, *c.* 1216;
16) *Petite philosophie,* c. 1225;
17) *Histoire de Marie et de Jésus;*
18) *Poème sur l'Ancien Testament;*
19) *Le Corset* and *Le Miroir,* by Robert de Gretham;
20) *Lumière as Lais,* by Pierre de Peckham, *c.* 1250; an Anglo-Norman redaction of *Image du monde, c.* 1250;
21) two Anglo-Norman versions of *Quatre soeurs* (Justice, Truth, Peace, Mercy), 13th century;
22) another *Comput* by Raüf de Lenham, 1256;
23) *Le chastel d'amors,* by Robert Grosseteste or Greathead, bishop of Lincoln;
24) *Poème sur l'amour de Dieu et sur la haine du péché,* 13th century, second part;
25) *Le mariage des neuf filles du diable;*

26) *Ditie d' Urbain,* attributed without any foundation to Henry I.

27) *Dialogue de l'évêque Saint Julien et son disciple;*

28) *Poème sur l'antichrist et le jugement dernier,* by Henri d'Arci;

29) Wilham de Waddington produced at the end of the 13th century his *Manuel des péchés,* which was adapted in England by Robert of Brunne in his *Handlying Sinne;*

In the 14th century these are found:

1) Nicole Bozon's *Contes moralisés;*

2) *Traité de naturesse;*

3) *Sermons* in verse;

4) *Proverbes de bon enseignement.*

Gautier de Biblesworth wrote such a treatise *à Madame Dyonise de Mountechensi pur aprise de langage; Orthographia gallica; La manière de language,* written in 1396; *Un petit livre pour enseigner les enfants de leur entreparler comun françois,* c. 1399.The important *Mirour de l'omme,* by John Gower, contains about 30,000 lines written in very good French at the end of the 14th century

Hagiography

Among the numerous lives of saints written in Anglo-Norman the most important ones are the following, the list of which is given in chronological order:

1) *Voyage de Saint Brandan* (or *Brandain*), written in 1121, by an ecclesiastic for Queen Aelis of Louvain;

2) Life of St. Catherine by Clemence of Barking;
3) Life of St Giles, c. 1170, by Guillaume de Berneville;
4) Life of St. Nicholas, life of Our Lady, by Wace; Uhlemann, *Gram. Krit. Studien zu Wace's Conception und Nicolas*, 1878;
5) Life of St. George by Simon de Fresne;
6) *Expurgatoire de Ste. Patrice*, by Marie de France;
7) *La vie de St. Edmund le Rei*, by Denis Pyramus, end of 12th century;
8) Henri d'Arci's life of St. Thais, poem on the Antichrist, *Visio S. Pauli*;
9) life of St. Gregory the Great by Frère Angier, 30 April 1214;
10) life of St. Modwenna, between 1225 and 1250;
11) Fragments of a life of St Thomas Becket, c. 1230; and another life of the same by Benoit of St. Alban, 13th century;
12) a life of Edward the Confessor, written before 1245, by an anonymous monk of Westminster; life of St. Auban, c. 1250.
13) *The Vision of Tnudgal*, an Anglo-Norman fragment, is preserved in MS. 312, Trinity College, Dublin; the MS. is of the 14th century; the author seems to belong to the 13th.

In this category the life of Hugh of Lincoln may be added, 13th century. Other lives of saints were recognised to be Anglo-Norman by Paul Meyer when examining the MSS. of the Welbeck library.

Lyric Poetry

The only extant songs of any importance are the seventy-one *Ballads* of Gower. The remaining songs are mostly of a religious character. Most of them have been discovered and published by Paul Meyer. Although so few have come down to us such songs must have been numerous at one time, owing to the constant intercourse between English, French and Provencals of all classes.

One of the finest productions of Anglo-Norman lyric poetry written in the end of the 13th century, is the *Plainte d'amour,* and may mention, merely as literary curiosities, various works of a lyrical character written in two languages, Latin and French, or English and French, or even in three languages, Latin, English and French.

Satire

The popularity enjoyed by the *Roman de Renart* and the Anglo-Norman version of the *Riote du Monde* in England is proof enough that the French spirit of satire was keenly appreciated. The clergy and the fair sex presented the most attractive target for the shots of the satirists. However, an Englishman raised his voice in favour of the ladies in a poem entitled *La Bonté des dames,* and Nicole Bozon, after having represented "Pride" as a feminine being whom he supposes to be the daughter of Lucifer, and after having fiercely attacked the women of his day in the *Char d'Orgueil,* also composed a *Bounté des femmes* in which he covers them with praise, commending their courtesy, their humility, their openness and the care with which they bring up their children. A few pieces of political satire show us French and English exchanging amenities on their mutual shortcomings. The *Roman des Français,* by André de Coutances, was written on the continent, and cannot be quoted as Anglo-Norman although it was composed before 1204. it is a very spirited reply to French authors who had attacked the English.

Drama

This must have had a considerable influence on the development of the sacred drama in England, but none of the French plays acted in England in the 12th and 13th centuries has been preserved. *Adam,* which is generally considered to be an Anglo-Norman mystery of the 12th century, was probably written in France at the beginning of the 13th century (*Romania* xxxii. 637), and the so-called Anglo-Norman *Resurrection* belongs also to continental French. It is necessary to state that the earliest English moralities seem to have been imitations of the French ones.

8

Medieval Byzantine Literature

Byzantine literature may be defined as the Greek literature of the Middle Ages, whether written in the territory of the Byzantine Empire or outside its borders. It forms the second period in the history of Greek literature, though *popular* Byzantine literature and early Modern Greek literature, which begin in the 11th century, are indistinguishable. A 11th Century Byzantine Gospel; its beautiful presentation perfectly illustrates the decorative style employed by scholars of that age.

Characteristics

Many of the classical Greek genres, such as drama and choral lyric poetry, had been obsolete by late antiquity, and all medieval literature in the Greek language was written in an archaising style, which imitated the writers of ancient Greece. This practice was perpetuated by a long-established system of Greek education where rhetoric was a leading subject. A typical product of this Byzantine education was the Greek Church Fathers, who shared the literary values of their pagan contemporaries. Consequently the vast Christian literature of the 3rd to 6th centuries established a synthesis of Hellenic and Christian thought. As a result, Byzantine literature was largely written in a style of Atticistic Greek, far removed from the popular Medieval Greek that was spoken by all classes of Byzantine society in their everyday lives. In addition, this literary style was also removed from the Koine Greek language of the New Testament, reaching back to Homer and the writers of ancient Athens.

In this manner, the culture of the Byzantine Empire was marked for over 1000 years by a diglossy between two different forms of the same language, which were used for different purposes. However, the relations between the "high" and "low" forms of Greek changed over the centuries. The prestige of the Attic literature remained undiminished until the 7th century AD, but in the following two centuries when the existence of the Byzantine Empire was threatened, city life and education declined, and along with them the use of the classicising language and style.

The political recovery of the 9th century instigated a literary revival, in which a conscious attempt was made to recreate the Hellenic-Christian literary culture of late antiquity. Simple or popular Greek was avoided in literary used and many of the early saints' lives were rewritten in an archaising style. By the 12th century the cultural confidence of the Byzantine Greeks lead them to develop new literary genres, such as romantic fiction, in which adventure and love are the main elements. Satire made occasional use of elements from spoken Greek.

The period from the Fourth Crusade to the Fall of Constantinople saw a vigorous revival of imitative classicising literature, as the Greeks sought to assert their cultural superiority over the militarily more powerful West. At the same time there was the beginning of a flourishing literature in an approximation to the vernacular Modern Greek. However the vernacular literature was limited to poetic romances and popular devotional writing. All serious literature continued to make use of the archaising language of learned Greek tradition.

Byzantine literature has two sources: Classical Greek and Orthodox Christian tradition. Each of those sources provided a series of models and references for the Byzantine writer and his readers. In occasion, both sources were referred to side by side, for example when emperor Alexius Comnenus justified his actions of seizing church property to pay his soldiers by referring to the earlier examples of Pericles and the biblical king David.

Greek

The oldest of these three civilisations is the Greek, centered not in Athens but in Alexandria and Hellenistic civilisation. Alexandria through this period is the center of both Atticising scholarship and of Graeco-Judaic social life, looking towards Athens as well as towards Jerusalem. This intellectual dualism between the culture of scholars and that of the people permeates the Byzantine period. Even Hellenistic literature exhibits two distinct tendencies, one rationalistic and scholarly, the other romantic and popular: the former originated in the schools of the Alexandrian sophists and culminated in the rhetorical romance, the latter rooted in the idyllic tendency of Theocritus and culminated in the idyllic novel. Both tendencies persisted in Byzantium, but the first, as the one officially recognised, retained predominance and was not driven from the field until the fall of the empire. The reactionary linguistic movement known as Atticism supported and enforced this scholarly tendency. Atticism prevailed from the second century B.C. onward, controlling all subsequent Greek culture, so that the living form of the Greek language was obscured and only occasionally found expression in private documents and popular literature.

Roman

Alexandria, the intellectual center, is balanced by Rome, the center of government. It is as a Roman Empire that the Byzantine state first entered history; its citizens were known as Romans (*Rhomaioi*), its capitol as New Rome (Constantinople). Its laws were Roman; so were its government, its army, and its official class, and at first also its language and its private and public life. The organisation of the state was very similar to that of the Roman imperial period, including its hierarchy and bureaucratic elite.

Christian

It was in Alexandria that Graeco-Oriental Christianity had its birth. There the Septuagint translation had been made; there that that fusion of Greek philosophy and Jewish religion took place which culminated in Philo; there flourished the mystic speculative neo-Platonism associated with Plotinus and Porphyry. At Alexandria the great Greek ecclesiastical writers worked alongside pagan rhetoricians and philosophers; several were born here, e.g. Origen, Athanasius, and his opponent Arius, also Cyril and Synesius. On Egyptian soil monasticism began and thrived. After Alexandria, Antioch held great prestige, where a school of Christian commentators flourished under St. John Chrysostom and where later arose the Christian universal chronicles. In surrounding Syria, we find the germs of Greek ecclesiastical poetry, while from neighboring Palestine came St. John of Damascus, the last of the Greek Fathers.

Oriental

Greek Christianity had of necessity a pronounced Oriental character; Ptolemaic Egypt and Seleucid Syria are the real birthplaces of the Graeco-Oriental church and Byzantine civilisation in general. Egypt and Syria, with Asia Minor, became for the autochthonous Greek civilisation a place where hundreds of flourishing cities sprang into existence, where energies confined or crippled in the impoverished homeland found release; not only did these cities surpass in material wealth the mother country, but soon also cultivated the highest goods of the intellect (Krumbacher). Under such circumstances it is not strange that about nine-tenths of all the Byzantine authors of the first eight centuries were natives of Egypt, Syria, Palestine, and Asia Minor.

Genres

The following account classifies Byzantine literature into five groups. The first three include representatives of those kinds of literature which continued the ancient traditions: historians and chroniclers, encyclopedists and essayists, and writers of secular poetry. The other two include new literary genres, ecclesiastical and theological literature, and popular poetry.

Historians and Annalists

The two groups of secular prose literature show clearly the dual character of Byzantine intellectual life in its social, religious, and linguistic aspects. From this point of view historical and annalistic literature supplement each other; the former is aristocratic and secular, the latter ecclesiastical and monastic; the former is classical, the latter popular. The works of the historians belong to scholarly literature, those of the annalists (or chroniclers) to the literature of the people. The former are carefully elaborated, the latter give only raw material, the former confine themselves to the description of the present and the most recent past, and thus have rather the character of contemporary records; the latter cover the whole history of the world as known to the Middle Ages. The former are therefore the more valuable for political history; the latter for the history of civilisation.

Historians

Classical literary tradition set the standard for Byzantine historians in their grasp of the aims of history, the manner of handling their subjects, and in style of composition. Their works are thoroughly concrete and objective in character, without passion, and even without enthusiasm. Ardent patriotism and personal convictions are rarely evident. They are diplomatic historians, expert in the use of historical sources and in the polished tact called for by their social position; they are not closet-scholars, ignorant of the world, but men who stood out in public life: jurists like Procopius, Agathias, Evagrius, Michael Attaliates, statesmen like Joannes Cinnamus, Nicetas Acominatus, Georgius Pachymeres, Laonicus Chalcondyles; generals and diplomats like Nicephorus Bryennius, George Acropolites, Georgius Phrantzes; and even crowned heads, like Constantine Porphyrogenitus, Anna Comnena, John VI Cantacuzene, and others. The Byzantine historians thus represent not only the social but also the intellectual flower of their time, resembling in this their Greek predecessors, Herodotus, Thucydides, Xenophon, and Polybius, who became their guides and models. Sometimes a Byzantine chooses a classic writer to imitate in method and style. The majority, however, took as models several authors, a custom which gave rise to a peculiar mosaic style, quite characteristic the Byzantines. While often the result of a real community of feeling, it effectively prevented development of an individual style.

Had such a preëminent historian as Procopius modeled his work after Polybius rather than Thucydides, Byzantine histories may have followed a natural continuity in style and method with the Hellenic era. The Hellenistic "Atticists" however had impressed their tastes thoroughly on later centuries, celebrating the style of the Athenian golden age. It is no accident that military characters like Nicephorus Bryennius (eleventh and twelfth centuries) and Joannes Cinnamus (twelfth century) emulated Xenophon in the precision of their diction, or that a philosopher like Nicephorus Gregoras (thirteenth century) took Plato as his model. On the other hand, it is doubtless due to chance that writers trained in theology like Leo Diaconus and Georgius Pachymeres chose to emulate Homeric turns. On the whole it is in the later historians that the dualism of Byzantine civilisation—ecclesiastico-political matter in classical form—becomes most apparent.

While Byzantine historians were mostly dependent on foreign models, and seem to form a continuous series in which each succeeds the last, they do not blend into a uniform whole. Most of the historians come in either the period embracing the sixth and seventh centuries during the reigns of the East-Roman emperors, or that extending from the eleventh to the fifteenth century under the Comneni and the Palaeologi. At its zenith under the Macedonian dynasty (the ninth and tenth centuries) the Byzantine world produced great heroes, but no great historians, excepting the solitary figure of the Emperor Constantine VII Porphyrogenitus.

The first period is dominated by Procopius because of his subject matter and his literary importance. Typically Byzantine, his *Anekdota* depreciates Emperor Justinian I as emphatically as his *Peri Ktismaton* apotheosizes him. In literature and history though, he follows classical models, as is evident in the precision and lucidity of his narrative acquired from Thucydides, and in the reliability of his information, qualities of special merit in the historian. Procopius and to a great degree his successor Agathias remain the models of descriptive style as late as the eleventh century. Procopius is the first representative of the ornate Byzantine style in literature and in this is surpassed only by Theophylaktos Simokattes in the seventh century. Despite their unclassical form, however, they approach the ancients in their freedom from ecclesiastical and dogmatic tendencies.

Between the historical writings of the first period and those of the second, there is an isolated series of works which in matter and form offer a strong contrast to both the aforesaid groups. These are the works under the name of the Emperor Constantine VII Porphyrogenitus (tenth century), dealing respectively with the administration of the empire, its political division, and the ceremonies of the Byzantine Court. They treat of the internal conditions of the empire, and the first and third are distinguished by their use of a popular tongue. The first is an important source of ethnological information, while the last is an interesting contribution to the history of civilisation.

The second group of historians present a classical eclecticism veiling an unclassical partisanship and theological fanaticism. Revelling in classical forms, the historians of the period of the Comneni and Palaeologi were devoid of the classical spirit. While many had stronger, more sympathetic personalities than the school of Procopius, the very vigor of these individuals and their close ties to the imperial government served to hamper their objectivity, producing subjective, partisan works.

Thus the "Alexiad", the pedantic work of Princess Anna Comnena, glorifies her father Alexius and the imperial reorganisation he began; the historical work of her husband, Nicephorus Bryennius, describes the internal conflicts that accompanied the rise of the Comneni in the form of a family chronicle (late eleventh century); John VI Cantacuzene self-complacently narrates his own achievements (fourteenth century).

This group exhibits striking antitheses both personal and objective. Beside Cinnamus, who honestly hated everything Western, stand the broad-minded Nicetas Acominatus (twelfth century) and the conciliatory but dignified Georgius Acropolites (thirteenth century); beside the theological polemicist

Pachymeres (thirteenth century), stands the man of the world, Nicephorus Gregoras (fourteenth century), well versed in philosophy and the classics. Though subjective in matters of internal Byzantine history, these and others of this period are trustworthy in their accounts of external events, and especially valuable as sources for the first appearance of the Slavs and Turks.

Chroniclers

Unlike the historical works, Byzantine chronicles were intended for the general public; hence the difference in their origin, development, and diffusion, as well as in their character, method, and style. While the roots of the chronicle have not yet been satisfactorily traced, their comparatively late appearance (sixth century) and total remove from Hellenistic tradition places their origins as fairly recent. The chronicle literature is originally foreign to Greek civilisation, the first of which was composed by uneducated Syrians. Its presumable prototype, the "Chronography" of Sextus Julius Africanus, points to an Oriental Christian source. Unconnected with persons of distinction and out of touch with the great world, it follows models bound within its own narrow sphere. The ninth century saw the zenith of the Byzantine chronicle, during the nadir of historical literature. Afterwards it declines abruptly; the lesser chroniclers, seen as late as the twelfth century, draw partly from contemporary and partly, though rarely, from earlier historians. In the Palaeologi period no chroniclers of note appear.

Not only important sources for the history of Byzantine civilization, the chronicles themselves contributed to the spread of civilisation, passing Byzantine culture to the arriving Slavic, Magyar, and

Turkic peoples. Depicting as they did what lay within the popular consciousness—events wonderful and dreadful painted in glaring colours and interpreted in a Christian sense—their influence was considerable. The method of handling materials is primitive—beneath each section lies some older source only slightly modified, so that the whole resembles a patchwork of materials rather than the ingenious mosaic of the historians. They are a rich store for comparative linguistics, as their diction is purely the popular tongue, bespeaking the poor education of author and audience.

Representative Byzantine chronicles are the three of Joannes Malalas, Theophanes Confessor, and Joannes Zonaras, respectively. The first is the earliest Christian Byzantine monastic chronicle, composed in the Antioch in the sixth century by a hellenised Syrian and Monophysite theologian. Originally a city chronicle, it was expanded into a world-chronicle. It is a popular historical work, full of historical and chronological errors, and the first monument of a purely popular Hellenistic civilisation. The chief source for most of the later chroniclers as well as for a few church historians, it is also the earliest popular history translated into Old Church Slavonic (ca. early tenth century). Superior in substance and form, and more properly historical, is the *Chronicle* of Theophanes, a ninth-century monk of Asia Minor, and in its turn a model for later chronicles. It contains much valuable information from lost sources, and its importance for the Western world is due to the fact that by the end of the ninth century it had to be translated into Latin. A third guide-post in the history of Byzantine chronicles is the twelfth-century *Universal Chronicle* of Zonaras. It reflects somewhat the atmosphere of the Comneni renaissance; not only is the narrative better than that of Theophanes, but many passages from ancient writers are worked into the text. It was translated not only into Slavic and Latin, but. into Italian and French as well (16th century).

Encyclopedists and Essayists

The spirit of antiquarian scholarship awoke in Byzantium earlier than in the West, but begun by lay theologians, not laymen. For this reason it always had a scholastic flavor; the Byzantine humanistic spirit savored of antiquity and the Middle Ages in equal proportion. Primarily directed to the systematic collection and sifting of manuscripts, a pronounced interest in the literature of Greek antiquity first manifested at Constantinople in the late ninth century. With the twelfth century begins the period of original works imitating antique models, a revival of the Alexandrian essay and rhetorical literature, a number of writers showing vigorous originality. Quite isolated between the two periods stands Michael Psellus (11th century), a universal genius who bridges the periods. While the humanism of the ninth and tenth centuries retained a theological coloring and a hostile attitude towards the West, the twelfth to the fourteenth century saw several writers seeking to break away from orthodox classicism to attain a true humanism, becoming the forerunners of the Italian Renaissance.

The new spirit first found expression in an academy founded for classical studies at Constantinople in 863. About the same time the broadly trained and energetic Photius, patriarch of the city and the greatest statesman of the Greek Church (820-897), enthusiastically collected forgotten manuscripts, revived forgotten works of antiquity, and re-discovered lost works; his attention was chiefly directed to prose works, indicative of his pragmatism. Photius made selections or excerpts from all the works he discovered, forming the beginning of his celebrated *Biblitheca* ("Library"), which while dry and schematic remains the most valuable literary compendium of the Middle Ages, containing trustworthy summaries of many ancient works now lost, together with good characterisations and analyses such as those of Lucian and Heliodorus. This encyclopedic activity was more assiduously pursued in the tenth century, particularly in the systematic collecting of materials associated with Emperor Constantine VII Porphyrogenitus. Scholars also formed great compilations, arranged by subject, on the basis of older sources: Among these was a now-fragmentary encyclopedia of political science containing extracts from the classical, Alexandrian, and Roman Byzantine periods. These, with the collection of ancient epigrams known as the *Anthologia Palatina* and the scientific dictionary known as the *Suidas*, make the tenth century that of the encyclopedias.

A typical representative of the period appears in the following century in the person of the greatest encyclopedist of Byzantine literature, Michael Psellus. Standing between the Middle Ages and modern times, he is a jurist and a man of the world with a mind both receptive and productive. Unlike Photius, who was more concerned with individual philosophic arguments, Psellus does not undervalue the old philosophers, and is himself of a philosophic temperament. Psellus was the first of his intellectual circle to raise the philosophy of Plato above that of Aristotle and to teach philosophy as a professor. Surpassing Photius in intellect and wit, he lacks that scholar's dignity and solidity of character. A restless brilliance characterised his life and literary activity. At first a lawyer, then a professor; now a monk, now a court official; ended his career the prime minister. Psellus was equally adroit and many-sided in his literary work; in harmony with the polished, pliant nature of the courtier is his elegant Platonic style of his letters and speeches. His extensive correspondence furnishes endless material illustrating his personal and literary character. The ennobling influence of his Attic models mark his speeches and especially his funerary orations; that delivered on the death of his mother shows deep sensibility. Psellus had more of a poetic temperament than Photius, as several of his poems show, though they owe more to satirical fancy and occasion than to deep poetic feeling. Though Psellus exhibits more formal skill than creativity, his endowments shone forth in a time particularly backward in aesthetic culture. The intellectual freedom of the great scholars (*polyhistores*), both ecclesiastical and secular, of the following centuries would be inconceivable without the triumph of Psellus over Byzantine scholasticism.

While among his successors—such as Nicephorus Blemmydes and Hyrtakenos—are natures as corrupt as Psellus' own, the majority are marked by their rectitude of intention, sincerity of feeling, and their beneficently broad culture. Among these great intellects and strong characters of the twelfth century several theologians are especially conspicuous, for example Eustathius of Thessalonica, Michael Italicus, and Michael Acominatus; in the thirteenth and fourteenth centuries several secular scholars, like Maximus Planudes, Theodorus Metochites, and above all, Nicephorus Gregoras.

The three theologians may best be judged by their letters and minor occasional writings. Eustathius seems to be the most important, writing learned commentary on Homer and Pindar alongside original works that are candid, courageous, and controversial, intent upon the correction of every evil. In one of his works he attacks the corruption and intellectual stagnation of the monastic life of that day; in another polemic, he assails the hypocrisy and sham holiness of his time; in a third he denounces the conceit and arrogance of the Byzantine priests.

The rhetorician Michael Italicus, later a bishop, attacks the chief weakness of Byzantine literature, external imitation; this he did on receiving a work by a patriarch, which was simply a disorderly collection of fragments from other writers, so poorly put together that the sources were immediately recognisable.

The pupil and friend of Eustathius, Michael Acominatus (twelfth and thirteenth centuries) Archbishop of Athens and brother of the historian Nicetas Acominatus. His inaugural address, delivered on the Acropolis, exhibits both profound classical scholarship and high enthusiasm despite the material and spiritual decay of his times. These pitiful conditions moved him to compose an elegy, famous because unique, on the decay of Athens, a sort of poetical and antiquarian apostrophe to fallen greatness. Gregorovius compared the inaugural address with Gregory the Great's to the Romans, and this with the lament of Bishop Hildebert of Tours on the demolition of Rome by the Normans (1106). His funeral orations over Eustathius (1195) and his brother Nicetas, though wordier and rhetorical, still evinced a noble disposition and deep feeling. Michael, like his brother, remained a fanatical opponent of the Latins. They had driven him into exile at Ceos, whence he addressed many letters to his friends illustrating his character. Stylistically influenced by Eustathius, his otherwise classical diction sounded an ecclesiastical note.

With Theodore Metochites and Maximos Planoudes come to the universal scholars (polyhistores) of the time of the Palaeologi. The former displays his humanism in his use of hexameter, the latter in his knowledge of the Latin; both of which are otherwise unknown in Byzantium, and foreboding a broader grasp of antiquity. Both men show a fine sense of poetry, especially of nature poetry. Metochites composed meditations on the beauty of the sea; Planudes was the author of a long poetic idyll, a genre uncultivated by Byzantine scholars. While Metochites was a thinker and poet, Planudes was chiefly an imitator and compiler.

Metochites was more speculative, as his collection of philosophical and historical miscellanies show; Planudes was more precise, as his preference for mathematics proves. Contemporary progress in philosophy was at a point where Metochites could openly attack Aristotle. Metochites deals more frankly with political questions, such as his comparison of democracy, aristocracy, and monarchy. While his breadth of interest was large, Metochites's culture rests wholly on a Greek basis, though Planudes, by his translations from the Latin (Cato, Ovid, Cicero, Caesar, and Boethius), vastly enlarged the Eastern intellectual horison.

This inclination toward the West is most noticeable in Nicephorus Gregoras, the great pupil of Metochites. His project for a reform of the calendar ranks him among the modern intellects of his time, as will be proven if ever his numerous works in every domain of intellectual activity are brought to light. His letters, especially, promise a rich harvest. His method of exposition is based on that of Plato, whom he also imitated in his ecclesiastico-political discussions, e.g. in his dialogue "Florentius, or Concerning Wisdom." These disputations with Barlaam dealt with the question of church union, in which Gregoras took the Unionist part. This brought him bitter hostility and the loss of his teaching living; he had been occupied chiefly with the exact sciences, whereby he had already earned the hatred of orthodox Byzantines.

While the Byzantine essayists and encyclopedists stood wholly under the influence of ancient rhetoric, still they embodied in the traditional forms their own characteristic knowledge, and thereby lent it a new charm.

Secular Poetry

Poetry likewise had its prototypes, each genre tracing its origins to an ancient progenitor. Unlike the prose, these new genres do not follow from the classical Attic period, for the Byzantines wrote neither lyrics nor dramas, imitating neither Pindar nor Sophocles. Imitating the literature of the Alexandrian period, they wrote romances, panegyrics, epigrams, satires, and didactic and hortatory poetry, following the models of Heliodorus and Achilles Tatius, Asclepiades and Posidippus, Lucian and Longus. Didactic poetry looks to an earlier prototype by pseudo-Isocrates. The poetic temperament of the Byzantines is thus akin to that of the Alexandrian writers. Only one new type evolved independently by the Byzantines—the begging-poem.

The six genres are not contemporaneous: the epigram and the panegyric developed first (sixth and seventh centuries), then, at long intervals, satire, next didactic and begging poetry, finally the romance. Only after the twelfth century, the period of decay, do they appear side by side. The epigram was the only form of secular poetry that had an independent revival in Byzantine literature, and this at the very time when ecclesiastical poetry also reached its highest perfection, in the sixth and seventh centuries. This age is therefore the most flourishing period of Byzantine scholarly poetry; its decline in the twelfth century is contemporary with the rise of popular poetry. The chief kinds of poetry during the period of the decline (eleventh to thirteenth century) were satire and parody, didactic and hortatory poetry, the begging-poem, and the erotic romance. In form the popular forms of speech and verse, the latter being the "political" verse, an iambic verse of fifteen syllables, still the standard verse of modern Greek popular poetry is characterised by its extensive use.

Epigram

The epigram suited the Byzantine taste for the ornamental and for intellectual ingenuity. It corresponded exactly to the concept of the minor arts that attained high development in the Byzantine period. Making no lofty demands on the imagination, its chief difficulty lay rather in technique and the attainment of the utmost possible pregnancy of phrase. Two groups may be distinguished among the Byzantine epigrammatists: one pagan and humanistic, the other Christian. The former is represented chiefly by Agathias (sixth century) and Christophorus of

Mitylene (eleventh century), the latter by the ecclesiastics Georgius Pisides (seventh century) and Theodorus Studites (ninth century). Between the two groups, in point of time as well as in character, stands Joannes Geometres (tenth century).

The chief phases in the development of the Byzantine epigram are most evident in the works of these three. Agathias, who has already been mentioned among the historians, as an epigrammatist, has the peculiarities of the school of the semi-Byzantine Egyptian Nonnus (about AD 400). Agathias wrote in an affected and turgid style, in the classical form of the hexameter; he abounds, however, in brilliant ideas, and in his skillful imitation of the ancients, particularly in his erotic pieces, he surpasses most of the epigrammatists of the imperial period. Agathias also prepared a collection of epigrams, partly his own and partly by other writers, some of which afterwards passed into the *Anthologia Palatina* and have thus been preserved.

The abbot Theodorus Studites is in every respect the opposite of Agathias, a pious man of deep earnestness, with a fine power of observation in nature and life, full of sentiment, warmth, and simplicity of expression, free from servile imitation of the ancients, though influenced by Nonnus. While touching on the most varied things and situations, his epigrams on the life and personnel of his monastery offer special interest for the history of civilisation. Joannes Geometres combines aspects of the previous two. During the course of his life he filled both secular and ecclesiastical offices and his poetry had a universal character; of a deeply religious temper, still he appreciated the greatness of the ancient Greeks.

Alongside epigrams on ancient poets, philosophers, rhetoricians, and historians stand others on famous Church Fathers, poets, and saints. Poetically, the epigrams on contemporary and secular topics are superior to those on religious and classic subjects. His best works depict historical events and situations he himself experienced, and reflect his own spiritual moods.

Panegyrics

Even the best writers often could not escape composing the official panegyrics on emperors and their achievements. Typical of this kind of literature are the commemorative poem of Paulus Silentiarius on the dedication of the church of St. Sophia, and that of Georgius Pisides on the glory of the prince. Unfavorable conclusions must not be drawn as to the character of these poets, for such eulogies were composed by not only courtiers like Psellus and Manuel Holobolos (thirteenth century), but also by independent characters like Eustathius and Michael Acominatus. It had become traditional, and so handed down from imperial Rome to Byzantium as a part of ancient rhetoric with all the extravagance of a thoroughly decadent literature. It was a sort of necessary concession to despotism; popular taste was not in general offended by it.

Satires

The father of Byzantine satire is Lucian. His celebrated "Dialogues of the Dead" furnished the model for two works, one of which, the "Timarion" (twelfth century) is marked by more rude humour, the other, "Mazaris" (fifteenth century), by keen satire. Each describes a journey to the underworld and conversations with dead contemporaries; in the former their defects are lashed with good-natured raillery; in the latter, under the masks of dead men, living persons and contemporary conditions, especially at the Byzantine Court, are sharply stigmatised. The former is more a literary satire, the latter a political pamphlet, with keen personal thrusts and without literary value, but with all the greater interest for the history of civilisation; the former is in a genuinely popular tone, the latter in vulgar and crude.

Two popular offshoots of the "Timarion", the "Apokopos" and the "Piccatoros" are discussed below. Another group of satires takes the form of dialogues between animals, manifestly a development from the Christian popular book known as the *Physiologus*. Such satires describe assemblages of quadrupeds, birds, and fishes, and recite their lampooning remarks upon the clergy, the bureaucracy, the foreign nations in the Byzantine Empire, etc.

Here belong also the parodies in the form of church poems, and in which the clergy themselves took part, e.g. Bishop Nicetas of Serrae (eleventh century). One example of this sacrilegious literature, though not fully understood, is the "Mockery of a Beardless Man," in the form of an obscene liturgy (fourteenth century).

Didactic

Didactic poetry found its model in the dialogue "To Demonikos", erroneously ascribed to Isocrates. The greatest example of this type of literature in Byzantium is the "Spaneas" (twelfth century), a hortatory poem addressed by an emperor to his nephew, a sort "Mirror for Princes". Some few offshots from this are found in the popular literature of Crete in the fifteenth and sixteenth centuries, handed down under the names of Sahlikis and Depharanus. Here also belong the ranting theological exhortations resembling those of the Capuchin in Schiller's "Wallenstein". Such, for instance, are that of Geogillas after the great plague of Rhodes (1498) and the oracular prophecies on the end of the Byzantine empire current under the name of Emperor Leo (886-911).

Begging-poem

A late Byzantine variety of the laudatory poem is the begging-poem, the poetical lament of hungry authors and the parasites of the court. Its chief representatives are Theodorus Prodromus and the grossly flattering Manuel Philes, the former of whom lived under the Comneni (twelfth century), the latter under the Palaeologi (thirteenth century). For historians such poetical wails of distress as Prodromus addressed to the emperor are of value because they give interesting pictures of street and business life in the capital.

Ecclesiastical and Theological Literature

The first flowering of ecclesiastical literature of Byzantium is Hellenistic in form and Oriental in spirit. This period falls in the fourth century and is closely associated with the names of the Greek Fathers of Alexandria, Palestine, Jerusalem, Cyrene, and Cappadocia. Their works, which cover the whole field of ecclesiastical prose literature—dogma, exegesis, and homiletics—became canonical for the whole Byzantine period; the last important work is the ecclesiastical history of Evagrius. Beyond controversial writings against sectarians and the Iconoclasts, later works consist merely of compilations and commentaries, in the form of the so-called *Catenae;* even the *Fountain of Knowledge* of John of Damascus (eighth century), the fundamental manual of Greek theology, though systematically worked out by a learned and keen intellect, is merely a gigantic collection of materials. Even the homily clings to a pseudo-classical, rhetorical foundation, and tends more to external breadth, not to inwardness and depth.

Only three kinds of ecclesiastical literature, which were as yet undeveloped in the fourth century, exhibit later an independent growth. These were the ecclesiastical poetry of the sixth century, popular lives of the saints of the seventh, and the mystic writings of the eleventh and twelfth centuries. The *Catholic Encyclopedia* suggests that classical forms were insufficient to express Christian thought to best effect: in several collections of early Christian correspondence it is not the rhythmic laws of Greek rhetorical style which govern the composition, but those of Semitic and Syriac prose. Cardinal Pitra hypothesises that the rhythmic poetry of the Byzantines originates in the Jewish Psalms of the Septuagint. This rhythmic principle accords with the linguistic character of the later Greek, which used a stress accent as it had already been developed in Syriac poetry rather than the classical tonal accent.

Romanos was the first great ecclesiastical poet of the Greeks to fully embrace the stress accent as a rhythmic principle. A contemporary and countryman of the chronicler Malalas, also a reformer of the Greek literary language, Romanos was a Syrian of Jewish descent, Christianised at an early age. What Malalas is to prose, Romanos is to the Christian poetry of the Greek Middle Ages. Though he did not go so far as Malalas, he released poetry from meters based on quantitative and tonal scansion; he brought it into harmony with the latest poetics prevailing in Syria as well as with the evolving character of the Greek language. Romanos soon went to Constantinople, where he became a deacon of the Hagia Sophia, and where he is said to have first developed his gift for hymn-writing.

Romanos borrowed the form of his poems, the material, and many of their themes partly from the Bible and partly from the (metrical) homilies of the Syrian Father Ephrem (fourth century). Romanos wrote hymns on the Passion of the Lord, on the betrayal by Judas, Peter's denial, Mary before the Cross, the Ascension, the Ten Virgins, and the Last Judgment, while his Old Testament themes mention the history of Joseph and the three young men in the fiery furnace. Romanos is said to have composed about a thousand hymns, of which only eighty have survived, evidently because in the ninth century the so-called *canones*, linguistically and metrically more artistic in form, replaced much of his work in the Greek Liturgy. Thenceforth his hymns held their own in only a few of the remoter monasteries.

Characteristic of his technique is the great length of his hymns, which are regularly composed of from twenty to thirty stansas (ôñïðáñéá) of from twelve to twenty-one verses each, very finely wrought and varied in metrical structure, and in construction transparent and diverse. They do not resemble contemporary Latin hymns so much as the oratorios of the early twentieth century, also using antiphonal rendering by alternative choirs. This also explains the dramatic character of many hymns, with their inserted dialogues and choric songs, as in "Peter's Denial", a little drama of human boastfulness and weakness, and the last part of the "History of Joseph", the "Psalm of the Apostles", and the "Birth of Jesus". Other pieces, like the hymn on the Last Judgment, are purely descriptive in character, though even in them the rhetorical and dogmatic elements seriously impair the artistic effect.

Some, like Bouvy and Krumbacher, place him among the greatest hymn-writers of all times; others, like Cardinal Pitra, are more conservative. For a final judgment a complete edition of the hymns is needed. Compared to Latin church poets such as Ambrose and Prudentius, his surviving works tend towards a more rhetorically flowery, digressive, and dogmatic verse. Romanos is fond of symbolic pictures and figures of speech, antitheses, assonances, especially witty *jeux d'esprit*, which contrast with his characteristic simplicity of diction and construction.

These embellishments interrupt the smooth flow of his lines, and often the sequence of thought in his hymns is clouded by the dragging in of dogmatic questions—in the celebrated Christmas hymn the question of the miraculous birth of Jesus is discussed four times, with a comfortable amplitude that betrays the theologian thrusting the poet aside.

The theologian is also too evident in his allusions to the Old Testament when dealing with New Testament incidents; Mary at the birth of Jesus compares her destiny to that of Sarah, the Magi liken the star that went before the Israelites in the wilderness, and so on. The frequent citation of passages from the prophets seem more like unimpassioned paraphrases than like inspired poetry. In fact Romanos does not possess the abundant and highly-coloured imagery of the earliest Greek church poets, nor their fine grasp of nature. The reader also gathers the impression that the height of the poet's imagination is not in proportion with the depth of his piety—there often appears in him something naive, almost homely, as when Mary expresses her pleasure in the Magi and calls attention to their utility for the impending Flight into Egypt. There are passages, however, in which devout fervor carries the imagination along with it and elevates the poetic tone, as in the jubilant invitation to the dance (in the Easter-song), in which thoughts of spring and of the Resurrection are harmoniously blended:

Why thus faint-hearted?
Why veil ye your faces?
Lift up your hearts!
Christ is arisen!
Join in the dances,
And with us proclaim it:
The Lord is ascended,
Gleaming and gloried,
He who was born
Of the giver of light.
Cease then your mourning,
Rejoice in blessedness:
Springtime has come.
So bloom now, ye lilies,
Bloom and be fruitful!
Naught bringeth destruction.
Clap we our hands
And shout: Risen is He
Who helpeth the fallen ones
To rise again.

Ecclesiastical poetry did not long remain on the high level to which Romanos had raised it. The "Hymnus Acathistus" (of unknown authorship) of the seventh century, a sort of Te Deum in praise of the Mother of God, is the last great monument of Greek church poetry, comparable to the hymns of Romanos, which it has even outlived in fame. It has had numerous imitators and as late as the seventeenth century was translated into Latin.

The rapid decline of Greek hymnology begins as early as the seventh century, the period of Andrew of Crete. Religious sentiments in hymns were choked by a classical formalism which stifled all vitality. The overvaluation of technique in details destroyed the sense of proportion in the whole. This seems to be the only explanation for the so-called canones first found in the collection of Andrew of Crete. While a canon is a combination of a number of hymns or chants (generally nine) of three or four strophes each, the "Great Canon" of Andrew actually numbers 250 strophes, a "single idea is spun out into serpentine arabesques".

Pseudo-classical artificiality found an even more advanced representative in John of Damascus, in the opinion of the Byzantines the foremost writer of canones, who took as a model Gregory of Nazianzus, even reintroducing the principle of quantity into ecclesiastical poetry. Religious poetry was in this way reduced to mere trifling, for in the eleventh century, which witnessed the decline of Greek hymnology and the revival of pagan humanism, Michael Psellus began parodying church hymns, a practice that took root in popular culture. Didactic poems took this form without being regarded as blasphemous.

Religious drama did not thrive in the Byzantine era. The only example is the *Suffering of Christ*, written in the eleventh or twelfth century; of its 2,640 verses, about one-third are borrowed from ancient dramas, chiefly from those of Euripides, and Mary, the chief character, sometimes recites verses from the "Medea" of Euripides, again from the "Electra" of Sophocles, or the "Prometheus" of Aeschylus. The composition is evidently the production of a theologian trained in the classics, but without the slightest idea of dramatic art. It is made up chiefly of lamentations and reports of messengers. Even the most effective scenes, those which precede the Crucifixion, are described by messengers; almost two-thirds of the text are given to the descent from the Cross, the lament of Mary, and the apparition of Christ.

Between ecclesiastical poetry and ecclesiastical prose stands the theologico-didactic poem, a favorite species of ancient Christian literature. One of its best examples is the "Hexaemeron" of Georgius Pisides, a spirited hymn on the universe and its marvels, i.e. all living creatures. Taken as a whole, it is somewhat conventional; only the description of the minor forms of life, especially of the animals, reveals the skill of the epigrammatist and nature-lover's gift of affectionate observation.

Besides sacred poetry, hagiography flourished from the sixth to the eleventh century. This species of literature developed from the old martyrologies, and became the favorite form of popular literature. It flourished from the eight to the eleventh century, and was concerned principally with monastic life. Unfortunately, the rhetorical language was in violent contrast with the simple nature of the contents, so that the chief value is historical.

More popular in style are the biographers of saints of the sixth and seventh centuries. The oldest and most important of them is Cyril of Scythopolis (in Palestine), whose biographies of saints and monks are distinguished for the reliability of their facts and dates. Of great interest also for their contributions to the history of culture and of ethics and for their genuinely popular language are the writings of Leontius, Archbishop of Cyprus (seventh century), especially his life of the Patriarch John (surnamed The Merciful), Eleemosynarius of Alexandria. This life describes for us a man who in spite of his peculiarities honestly tried "to realise a pure Biblical Christianity of self-sacrificing love", and whose life brings before us in a fascinating way the customs and ideas of the lower classes of the people of Alexandria.

The romance of Balaam and Joasaph (also Barlaam and Josaphat) was another popular work of Byzantine origin now elevated to universal literature. It is the "Song of Songs" of Christian asceticism, illustrated by the experience of the Indian prince Joasaph, who is led by the hermit Barlaam to abandon the joys of life, and as a true Christian to renounce the world. The material of the story is originally Indian, indeed Buddhistic, for the origin of Joasaph was Buddha. The Greek version originated in the Sabbas monastery in Palestine about the middle of the seventh century. It did not circulate widely until the eleventh century, when it became known to all Western Europe through the medium of a Latin translation.

The ascetic conception of life was embedded in the Byzantine character and was strengthened by the high development of monastic institutions. The latter in turn brought forth a broad ascetic literature, though it does not further deepen the asceticism of its great exponent, St. Basil of Caesarea.

Less extensively cultivated, but excelling in quality, are Byzantine mystical writings. The true founder of a distinctively *Byzantine* mysticism was Maximus the Confessor (seventh century), who deepened the tradition of Christian Neo-Platonism, as found in the Pseudo-Dionysius, with the resources of Orthodox Christology. No other writer in Eastern Christian tradition surpasses Maximus in speculative range and originality. Later representatives of this mystical tradition were Symeon the New Theologian and Nicetas Stethatos in the eleventh, and Nikolaos Kavasilas in the fourteenth century.

The Byzantine mystical writers differ from those of Western Europe chiefly in their attitude to ecclesiastical ceremonies, to which they adhered implicitly, seeing in it a profound symbol of the spiritual life of the church, where Occidentals see an attempt to displace the inner life with external pomp. Accordingly Symeon strictly observed the ceremonial rules of the church, regarding them, however, only as a means to the attainment of ethical perfection. His principal work (published only in Latin) is a collection of prose pieces and hymns on communion with God.

Symeon is akin to the chief German mystics in his tendency towards pantheism. Of Symeon's equally distinguished pupil, Nicetas Stethatos, the only need to say that Symeon cast off his teacher's pantheistic tendencies. The last great mystic Kavasilas, Archbishop of Saloniki, revived the teaching of Dionysius the Pseudo-Areopagite, but in the plan of his principal work, "Life in Christ", exhibits a complete independence of all other worlds and is without a parallel in Byzantine asceticism.

Popular Poetry

The capture of Constantinople and establishment of the Latin kingdoms in the year 1204 displaced or supplanted aristocratic and ecclesiastic controls on literary taste and style. In response to new influences from the Roman West, Byzantine popular literature moved in different directions. Whereas literary poetry springs from the rationalistic, classical atmosphere of the Hellenistic period, popular poetry, or folk-song, is an outgrowth of the idyllic, romantic literature of the same period. As the literary works had their prototypes in Lucian, Heliodorus, Achilles Tatius, and Nonnus, the popular works imitated Apollonius of Rhodes, Callimachus, Theocritus, and Musaeus.

The chief characteristic of folk-song throughout the Greek Middle Ages is its lyric note, which constantly finds expression in emotional turns. In Byzantine literature, on the other hand, the refinement of erotic poetry was due to the influence of the love-poetry of chivalry introduced by Frankish knights in the thirteenth century and later. The Byzantines imitated and adapted the romantic and legendary materials these westerners brought. Italian influences led to the revival of the drama. That celebration of the achievements of Greek heroes in popular literature was the result of the conflicts which the Greeks sustained during the Middle Ages with the border nations to the east of the empire. Popular books relating the deeds of ancient heroes had long-standing and widespread currency throughout the East; these too revived heroic poetry, though imparted with a deep romantic tinge. The result was a complete upheaval of popular ideals and a broadening of the popular horizon as Atticist tendencies were gradually eroded.

There was, consequently, a complete reconstruction of the literary types of Byzantium. Of all the varieties of artistic poetry there survived only the romance, though this became more serious in its aims, and its province expanded. Of metrical forms there remained only the political (fifteen-syllable) verse. From these simple materials there sprang forth an abundance of new poetic types. Alongside of the narrative romance of heroism and love there sprang up popular love lyrics, and even the beginnings of the modern drama.

The only genuine heroic epic of the Byzantines is the "Digenis Acritas", a popular poetic crystallisation of the tenth- and eleventh-century conflicts between the Byzantine wardens of the marches and the Saracens in Eastern Asia Minor. The nucleus of this epic goes back to the twelfth or thirteenth century, its final literary form to the fifteenth. Though the schoolmen edited the original poems beyond recognition, an approximate idea of the original poem may be gathered from the numerous echoes of it extant in popular poetry.

The existing versions exhibit a blending of several cycles, modeled after the Homeric poems. Its principal subjects are love, adventures, battles, and a patriarchal, idyllic enjoyment of life; it is a mixture of the Iliad and the Odyssey, the majority of the material being drawn from the latter, suffused with a Christian atmosphere. Genuine piety and a strong family feeling combine with an intimate sympathy with nature. Artistically, the work lacks the dramatic quality and diverse characters of the Germanic and classical Greek epics; it must be compared with the Slavic and Oriental heroic songs, among which it properly belongs.

The love-romance of the Greek Middle Ages is the result of the fusion of the sophistical Alexandro-Byzantine romance and the medieval French popular romance, on the basis of a Hellenistic view of life and nature. This is proved by its three chief creations, composed in the thirteenth and fourteenth centuries. "Kallimachos and Chrysorrhoe", "Belthandros and Chrysantza", "Lybistros and Rhodamne". While the first and the last of these are markedly influenced by Byzantine romance in thought and manner of treatment, the second begins to show the aesthetic and ethical influence of the Old-French romance; indeed, its story often recalls the Tristan legend.

The style is clearer and more transparent, the action more dramatic, than in the extant versions of the Digenis legend. The ethical idea is the romantic idea of knighthood—the winning of the loved one by valour and daring, not by blind chance as in the Byzantine literary romances. Along with these independent adaptations of French material, are direct translations from "Flore et Blanchefleur", "Pierre et Maguelonne", and others, which have passed into the domain of universal literature.

To the period of Frankish conquest belongs also the metrical Chronicle of Morea (fourteenth century). It was composed by a Frank brought up in Greece, though a foe of the Greeks. Its object was, amid the constantly progressing hellenisation of the Western conquerors, to remind them of the spirit of their ancestors. Therefore it is only Greek in language; in literary form and spirit it is wholly Frankish.

About the same time and in the same locality the small islands off the coast of Asia Minor, appeared the earliest collection of neo-Greek love songs, known as the "Rhodian Love-Songs". Besides songs of various sorts and origins, they contain a complete romance, told in the form of a play on numbers, a youth being obliged to compose a hundred verses in honor of the maiden whom he worships before she returns his love, each verse corresponding to the numbers one to one hundred.

Between the days of the French influence in the thirteenth and fourteenth centuries and those of Italian in the sixteenth and seventeenth, there was a short romantic and popular revival of the ancient legendary material. There was neither much need nor much appreciation for this revival, and few of the ancient heroes and their heroic deeds are adequately treated. The best of these works is the *Alexander Romance,* based on the story of Alexander the Great, a revised version of the Pseudo-Callisthenes of the Ptolemaic period, which is also the source of the western versions of the *Alexander Romance.* The "Achilleis", on the other hand, though written in the popular verse and not without taste, is wholly devoid of antique local colour, and is rather a romance of French chivalry than a history of Achilles. Lastly, of two compositions on the Trojan War, one is wholly crude and barbarous, the other, though better, is a literal translation of the old French poem of Benoît de Sainte-More.

To these products of the fourteenth century may be added two of the sixteenth, both describing a descent into the lower world, evidently popular offshoots of the Timarion and Mazaris already mentioned. To the former corresponds the "Apokopos", a satire of the dead on the living; to the latter the "Piccatores", a metrical piece decidedly lengthy but rather unpoetic, while the former has many poetical passages (e.g. the procession of the dead) and betrays the influence of Italian literature. In fact Italian literature impressed its popular character on the Greek popular poetry of the sixteenth and seventeenth centuries, as French literature had done in the thirteenth and fourteenth.

Cretan Popular Poetry

As a rich popular poetry sprang up during the last-mentioned period on the islands off the coast of Asia Minor, so now a similar literature developed on the Island of Crete. Its most important creations are the romantic epic "Erotokritos" and the dramas "Erophile" and "The Sacrifice of Abraham" with a few minor pictures of customs and manners. These works fall chronologically outside the limits of Byzantine literature; nevertheless, as a necessary complement and continuation of the preceding period, they should be discussed here.

The "Erotokritos" is a long romantic poem of chivalry, lyric in characters and didactic in purpose, the work of Cornaro, a hellenised Venetian of the sixteenth century. It abounds in themes and ideas drawn from the folk-poetry of the time. In the story of Erotokritos and Arethusa the poet glorifies love and friendship, chivalric courage, constancy, and self-sacrifice. Although foreign influences do not obtrude themselves, and the poem, as a whole, has a national Greek flavour, it reveals the various cultural elements, Byzantine, Romance, and Oriental, without giving, however, the character of a composite.

The lyrical love tragedy "Erophlle" is more of a mosaic, being a combination of two Italian tragedies, with the addition of lyrical intermezsos from Torquato

Tasso's "Jerusalem Delivered", and choral songs from his "Aminta". Nevertheless, the materials are handled with independence, and more harmoniously arranged than in the original; the father who has killed his daughter's lover is slain not by his daughter's hand, but by the ladies of his palace, thus giving a less offensive impression. Owing to the lyric undertone of the works some parts of it have survived in popular tradition until the present time.

The mystery play of "The Sacrifice of Abraham" is a little psychological masterpiece, apparently an independent work. The familiar and trite Biblical incidents are reset in the patriarchal environment of Greek family life. The poet emphasises the mental struggles of Sarah, the resignation of Abraham to the Divine will, the anxious forebodings of Isaac, and the affectionate sympathy of the servants, in other words, a psychological analysis of the characters. The mainspring of the action is Sarah's fore-knowledge of what is to happen, evidently the invention of the poet to display the power of maternal love. The diction is distinguished by high poetic beauty and by a thorough mastery of versification.

Other products of Cretan literature are a few adaptations of Italian pastorals, a few erotic and idyllic poems, like the so-called "Seduction Tale", and the lovely, but ultra-sentimental, pastoral idyll of the "Beautiful Shepherdess".

Legacy of Byzantine Literature

The Roman supremacy in governmental life did not disappear, amplified as it was by its union with the Eastern despotic traditions of rulership. The subjection of the Church to the power of the State led to a governmental ecclesiasticism, causing friction with Roman Catholic Church, which had remained relatively independent.

Greek eventually overtook Latin as the official language of the government, the "Novellae" of Justinian I being the last Latin monument. As early as the seventh century Greek language had made great progress, and by the eleventh Greek was supreme, though it never supplanted the numerous other languages of the empire. While the Greek world preserved the form of its classical literature, the same cannot be said of the classical sense of poetry and imagination. The Byzantine culture broke completely with the classical aesthetic; in literature and in the plastic arts the Oriental aesthetic was victorious.

Some genres such as lyric verse and drama died out, while only in the minor departments of literature was any great degree of skill attained. The classical sense of proportion, beauty, and poetry disappear completely, replaced by a delight in the grotesque and the disproportioned on the one hand, and in ornamental trifles on the other.

Social conditions, more of the East than of classical Athenian/Roman culture, encouraged these aesthetic trends.

The loss of a body of free, educated citizens to Byzantine centralisation and the consequent stagnation of municipal life directly affected its literature. No rivals were permitted to Constantinople. Literature concerned only the high official and priestly classes; it was aristocratic or theological rather than popular. Classical standards could be imitated because only the upper classes concerned themselves with literature, but, divorced from the life of the people, it lacked genuine spontaneity. Church hymnology for some time infused fresh life into literature, but even this was of Oriental origin, growing out of Syria. In Byzantium, ecclesiastical and Eastern influences coincided.

The Eastern Roman Empire divided European civilisation into two parts: one Romance and Germanic, the other Greek and Slavic. These cultures differed ethnographically, linguistically, ecclesiastically, and historically. Imperial Russia, the Balkans, and Ottoman Empire were the direct heirs of Byzantine civilisation; the first two particularly in ecclesiastical, political, and cultural respects (through the translation and adaptation of sacred, historical, and popular literature); the third in respect to civil government.

Indirectly, the Empire protected western Europe for centuries from war, fighting off various invaders and migratory populations. Byzantium was also a treasury of ancient Greek literature. During the Middle Ages, until the capture of the Constantinople, the West was acquainted only with Roman literature. Greek antiquity was first carried to Italy by the treasures brought by fugitive Greek humanists, many of whom were delegates at the Council of Florence from 1331 to 1346.

Byzantine culture had a direct influence upon southern and central Europe in church music and church poetry, though this was only in the very early period (until the seventh century).

Byzantine culture had a definite impact upon the Near East, especially upon the Armenians, the Persians, and the Arabs.

9

Medieval Spanish Literature

Medieval English literature made its way into Spanish long before the current began to flow in the other direction: though it is possible that Chaucer came across Juan Ruiz' Libro de Buen Amor when he was in Spain in 1366, it was not until the late 1520s and early 1530s that translations and adaptations began, the first being Fernando de Rojas' dialogue novel Tragicomedia de Calisto y Melibea and Diego de San Pedro' sentimental romance Cárcel de Amor.

John Rastell translated the first acts of Celestina and equipped them with a happy ending, publishing A New Cõmodye in Englysh in Maner of an Enterlude *c.*1530. The first extant translation of the complete work is by James Mabbe (1572–*c.*1642), whose The Spanish Bawd was published in 1631. Mabbe' work has been used as the basis for a number of stage and radio productions. Mabbe' style is ornate, but his book still reads well, in some ways better than his 20th-c. successors. In two respects The Spanish Bawd falsifies its original: some sexually explicit phrases are smoothed over, and the Catholic setting (invocations of God and the Virgin, references to the Mass) is, in deference to Protestant sensibilities, replaced by classical mythology. These changes are now known to belong to the second phase of Mabbe' translation. The first phase, a manuscript version from the first decade of the century, is much closer to the Spanish.

Probably at the same time as Rastell was working on his Enterlude, John Bourchier, Lord Berners (1467–*c.*1533) translated Cárcel de Amor and its short sequel (1495) by Nicolás Núñez. Berners used a French translation as the basis for his own, correcting it from the Spanish, but for Núñez' sequel he worked directly from the Spanish. He is for C. S. Lewis 'the last of the great medieval translators ... Malory' equal' (Lewis 1954). His posthumously published translation is riddled with errors, but he gives a fair impression of San Pedro' style, and his book had a considerable influence on the evolution of Elizabethan prose style. San Pedro' first romance, Arnalte y Lucenda (*c.*1481), though not of the same quality as Cárcel de Amor, rivalled it in European popularity and far surpassed it in English. The translation by the Catholic apologist John Clerk, from Nicolas d'Herberay' French, published in 1543, was followed by three other versions, two of them greatly changed, by different hands between 1575 and 1660.

Although the first of the Spanish sentimental romances, Juan Rodríguez del Padrón' Siervo libre de amor (*c.*1440, Love' Free Slave), was never rendered into English, Juan de Flores' Grisel y Mirabella (*c.*1480) appeared in 1556 in a quadrilingual edition (French, Italian, Spanish-a retranslation from the Italian—and English). Like other editions of sentimental romances this proved popular, and it was reprinted four times. Another, much freer version was printed in 1606. Thus eight translations or free adaptations of sentimental romances were printed, in 17 editions, between 1543 and 1660. The vogue for this genre in England was soon reinforced by the demand for translations of chivalresque and pastoral romances, and the growing interest in Celestina was accompanied by the popularity of the picaresque novels.

Late medieval Spanish fiction played a decisive part in the formation of Elizabethan taste and of the English novel, and not always through translations. The neo-Arthurian romance Amadís de Gaula (c.1495) was known in Elizabethan England well before the pamphleteer and dramatist Anthony Munday (1553–1633) published the first volume of his translation in 1590: Queen Elizabeth was already being called Oriana in the 1560s.

In 1567 Thomas Paynell (d. 1576), sometime chaplain to Henry VIII, translated from French a florilegium of speeches and letters from Amadís and its sequels, and in 1571 Charles Stewart, son of the Regent of Scotland, began to translate the first book (he soon abandoned his task). Thus Anthony Munday' The Ancient, Famous and Honourable History of Amadis de Gaule (published between 1590 and 1619, so in its later stages contemporary with Shelton' Don Quixote) was a response to an already established fashion. Munday worked from the French of Nicolas d'Herberay, who had amplified both the style and the content of the Spanish original, making it more rhetorical and adding erotic scenes.

Munday, who elsewhere translated rather freely, in this work followed Herberay closely. The double process of translation inevitably leads away from the sense of the original at times, but the style is good, and this is still a readable romance.

Spanish poetry was much read in the England of the Tudors, and in Stuart Scotland and England, but it was not much translated. A curious exception is the version of the Proverbios of íñigo López de Mendoza, Marquis of Santillana, with the glosses of the scholar Pero Díaz de Toledo. The Proverbios (1437) is a moral poem designed as a speculum principis for the heir to the Castilian throne. In the translation by the poet Barnabe Googe (1540–94) a century and a half later, it clearly had its relevance for Elizabethan England.

Translations of medieval Spanish works in the early 18th c. are a continuation of the previous century' work: John Shirley abridged Munday' Amadís in 1702, and five years later two versions of Celestina, one narrative and the other dramatic, appeared simultaneously. Captain John Stevens, translator and historian, included The Bawd of Madrid in a collection of four works (two of them picaresque novels), and an anonymous author or authors published Celestina: or, the Spanish Bawd, A Tragi-Comedy with another picaresque novel. Both are free versions, Stevens' throughout and the anonymous play in its second half. The Tragi-Comedy seems to adapt Mabbe' Spanish Bawd, but Stevens seems to have worked directly from the Spanish.

Until the beginning of the 19th c., English translators showed interest only in late medieval Spanish literature. It fell to Robert Southey (1774–1843) to make earlier works available to English-speaking readers. He had already published an abridged translation of Amadís de Gaula in 1803; it was reviewed in the same year by Walter Scott, whose own romances may have been influenced by Amadís and its successors. In 1808 he published The Chronicle of the

Cid, a composite work mainly derived from the Chrónica del famoso cavallero Cid Ruy Díaz Campeador, a late medieval reworking of parts of the Estoria de España planned and directed by Alfonso X, the Wise, King of Castile 1252–84. Southey supplemented this by direct recourse to the Estoria de España and to the early 13th-c. epic the Poema de Mio Cid. The result is a splendid narrative, in a style that conveys the spirit of a vanished age while avoiding excessive archaism. V. S. Pritchett calls him 'one of the great masters of plain, flowing, and conversable prose narrative in our language'.

No full translation of the Poema de Mio Cid was to come for nearly 80 years, but Southey had opened up Spain' earlier medieval literature, and his example was followed. His predecessors had translated, retranslated, or adapted what was to them more or less contemporary literature. Southey did not (unlike Thomas Percy) use the term 'ancient poetry', but he knew that he was interpreting a bygone age.

Southey did not think highly of Spanish ballads ('infinitely and every way inferior to our own'), and he made only a little use of them in his Chronicle, but before long other translators rightly took a different view: Scott' biographer, the novelist John Gibson Lockhart (1794–1854), the traveller, MP, and hymn-writer Sir John Bowring (1792–1872), and the Scottish clergyman and prolific translator from Spanish and German James Young Gibson (1826–86).

Henry Wadsworth Longfellow, Professor of Modern Languages at Harvard as well as the poet of Hiawatha, was captivated by some Spanish poems, recreating 'the Spanish ballad | of the noble Count Arnaldos' in The Secret of the Sea (1849). This was not

Longfellow' first venture into medieval Spanish: in 1832 he had published in a magazine a version of Jorge Manrique' Coplas por la muerte de su padre (1479, Verses for His Father' Death), at once elegy and moral reflection, the one poem (apart from ballads) of 15th-c. Castile that is still widely read today. Longfellow' version is, like The Secret of the Sea, re-creation rather than strict translation, and though there have in recent decades been accurate published translations, none really fills the gap.

In the last quarter of the 19th c., what we may regard as modern translations from medieval Spanish begin, some aimed at the general reader, while in others the concept of a scholarly translation is dominant. Some older translations are reprinted or adapted (but often with a substantial introduction), but in the new ones accuracy is increasingly seen to be as important as readability. Moreover, the range of works made available is steadily widened: the first (though old-fashioned and unreliable) version of Juan Manuel' exemplum collection, El Conde Lucanor (1335), was published in 1868 and the first full translation of the Poema de Mio Cid in 1879.

In 1882 the folklorist Henry Charles Coote (1815–85) appended to his translation of a monograph on the Seven Sages his English rendering (Book of the Deceits and Tricks of Women) of the Libro de los engaños (*c.*1253), the first substantial translation addressed primarily to scholars, and his example was soon followed. The second version of the Poema de Mio Cid (in verse, like the first) was published in 1897–1903, with an edition of the Spanish original and extensive notes, by the bibliophile and founder of the Hispanic Society of America, Archer M. Huntington.

20th-c. translations of medieval Spanish literature are numerous. Many works, including some of the major ones, have not been translated, but many have. The audience addressed varies: students, comparatists, the educated general reader-or, of course, more than one of these. In one remarkable case, a specialist audience is addressed for a practical reason: some of the laws in the Siete partidas, the encyclopedic legal code of Alfonso the Wise, are still in force in Louisiana, so partial translations were published in New Orleans in 1819–20, and over a century later the Comparative Law Bureau of the American Bar Association commissioned Samuel Parsons Scott to produce a full translation of this massive work.

Sometimes translations are inept, but more often they are serviceable, and a few are excellent: for instance, Joan Evans' abridgement of El Victorial (early 1430s), a blend of chronicle, biography, and travel-book (1928), Keith Whinnom' translation of two sentimental romances by San Pedro and Nuñez, which combines accuracy with a fine sense of the cadences of the original, and Roger Wright' rendering of some 70 ballads (facing the originals) into English couplets. Wright chooses fidelity to the meaning rather than to the words; his versions are splendid performance texts.

The works most often translated are the Poema de Mio Cid, Celestina, the best-known ballads, and Juan Ruiz'. Libro de Buen Amor. The last, despite its importance, is a late starter; the first generally available translation—by Rigo Mignani and Mario A. Di Cesare—did not appear until 1970 (it was followed by three others in the next eight years). Both this and the next translation, by Raymond S. Willis, use prose for the alexandrine lines of most of the original and verse for the inset lyrics, but they differ sharply in their aim: Mignani and Di Cesare give precedence to clarity and fidelity to the original, and their translation is designed to be read on its own, while Willis describes his version as a paraphrase (he sometimes omits a line), 'exclusively ... an aid to understanding the Spanish'.

The first three translators of the Poema de Mio Cid (between 1879 and 1919) used verse, but their successors generally used prose, a striking exception being the American poet W. S. Merwin, whose poem reads splendidly, though sometimes at the expense of accuracy. The prose translation by Rita Hamilton and Janet Perry, now much the most widely known, is both readable and accurate, its only flaw being that epic epithets and other repeated phrases are sometimes omitted.

It has proved surprisingly difficult to achieve a successful modern English Celestina, and the great majority of the numerous stage and radio productions over the past 50 years have used adaptations of James Mabbe. There were five translations in the 1950s and 1960s; J. M. Cohen' for Penguin Classics is the most widely known, but Phyllis Hartnoll' for Everyman' Library is clearly the best: though lacking Mabbe' vigour, it is both accurate and readable.

Space allows only the briefest mention of good recent translations of other important works. Gonzalo de Berceo' mid-13th-c. Milagros de Nuestra Señora does not go well into English verse, so Richard Terry Mount and Annette Grant Cash have solved the problem with a prose translation broken up into lines that correspond to the original. A similar method is used by T. A. Perry for the mid-14th-c. Proverbios morales of Rabbi Sem Tob. There are two translations of Juan Manuel' El Conde Lucanor, of which John England' is the more successful, and Alfonso Martínez de Toledo' Arcipreste de Talavera (1438), part pungently written treatise, part collection of anecdotes, is effectively rendered by Lesley Byrd Simpson. Other works have been usefully translated: John Esten Keller has not only produced versions of several exemplum collections but has encouraged colleagues to translate Amadís de Gaula and the first indigenous Spanish romance, El libro del cavallero Zifar.

There are still gaps, most obviously the major 13th-c. poems written in cuaderna vía, monorhymed alexandrine quatrains; the Mount and Cash Miracles of Our Lady is the first successful translation published in this area. Yet despite the gaps, English-speaking readers now have at least one adequate (or better) translation of most of the major works of medieval Spanish literature, and in some cases they have a choice of versions. They are not necessarily restricted to books: it is probable that more people have heard Celestina in English on the radio or seen it on the stage than have read all of the translations put together; and it is certain that-despite the availability of good translations of the Poema de Mio Cid- the majority of English-speakers owe their familiarity with the hero to the Charlton Heston film.

Early Spanish Literature and the Middle Ages

The Jarchas

It was believed that the first Ibero-Romance literature began with the anonymous epic poem, the *Poema del Cid*, written around 1140AD. However, in 1948, Hebrew scholar Samuel M. Stern published 24 *jarchas*, "short lyric poems written in very archaic Spanish," which he had found in a synagogue in Cairo. Stern and Spanish scholar Emilio García Gómez later found more jarchas, and since 1948 their sum total is over fifty. The jarcha is usually the lament of a lower-class woman for her absent sweetheart. It is the final three- or four-lined stanza of the muwashshah, a form of verse used by Arabic and Hebrew poets from the eleventh to the thirteenth century.

The jarcha is written in Mozarabic, a Romance language spoken by the majority of the population during this period. Because the Arabic and Hebrew characters lacked certain vowel signs, scholars have trouble transliterating the jarchas. The lack of knowledge of the Mozarabic language also hinders interpretations. Nonetheless, it is now widely accepted that Mozarabic was a separate Romance language which evolved directly from Vulgar Latin, not from Castilian Spanish.

Cantar de Mio Cid

The Cantar de Mio Cid was written about a real man—his battles, conquests, and daily life. The poet, name unknown, wrote the epic in about 1140 and Cid supposedly died forty years before in 1099. This epic represents realism, because nothing was exaggerated and the details are very real, even the geography correctly portrays the areas in which Cid traveled and lived. Unlike other European epics, the poem is not idealized and there is no presence of supernatural beings. It has assonance instead of rhyme and its lines vary in length, the most common length being fourteen syllables. This type of verse is known as *mester de juglaria* (verse form of the minstrels). The epic is divided into three parts, also known as cantos.

— *Part I* is about Ruy Diaz de Vivar, who is called Cid (meaning my Lord) by the Moors. His current task is to collect the tributes from the Moorish territory owed to his king, Alfonso VI of Leon. Cid's enemy accuses him of taking some of these tributes and the king exiles him from Leon and Castilla. Before he leaves, he places his wife, Doña Jimena, and his two daughters, Doña Elvira and Doña Sol, in the Monastery of Cardeña. The canto then accounts of raids in the Moorish territory in which Cid and his men get rich off of the spoils.

— *Part II* begins with Cid's capture of the city of Valencia. He brings his family to live with him. It is discovered that the Infantes (princes) de Carrión, the nephews to the king, are the enemies who caused Cid's exile. They plot to marry his daughters to take some of his wealth. The king acts on behalf of his nephews and pardons Cid and allows the marriages. Cid suspects that something bad will happen from the marriages.

— *Part III* shows that the Infantes are cowards in battles with the Moors. They are made fun of and decided to get revenge by attacking their wives. They set out for Carrión with their wives and an escort, Felix Muñoz, the cousin of the daughters. Once on the journey, they send the escort ahead of them, steal their wives' great dowries (including two beautiful swords) and beat them and leave them for dead. Muñoz suspects trouble and returns to his cousins and takes them to receive help. Cid seeks to right the wrongs done to his daughters and a trial is held. A duel is held between some of Cid's men and the Infantes in which the Infantes lose. In the middle of the trial, a message was sent from the kings of Navarra and Aragon, proposing to marry their sons to Cid's daughters. These marriages take place after the defeat of the Infantes.

Mester de Juglaría

Medieval Spanish poets recognized the Mester de Juglaría as a literary form written by the minstrels (juglares) and composed of varying line length and use of assonance instead of rhyme. These poems were sung to uneducated audiences, nobles and peasants alike.

Mester de Clerecía

This Castilian narrative poetry known as the Mester de Clerecía became popular in the thirteenth century. It is the verse form of the learned poets, usually clerics (hence the name 'clerecía'). These poets carefully counted the number of syllables in each line and strived to achieve perfect lines. The line form is the Alexandrine line (14 syllables) with consonantal rhyme in stanzas of four lines each. This form is also known as the *cuaderna vía* or the fourfold way, and was borrowed from France and was popular until the late fourteenth century. Popular themes of these poets were: Christian legends, lives of saints, and tales from classical antiquity.

The poems were cited to villagers in public plazas. Two traits separate this form from the mester de juglaría: didacticism and erudition. Castilian priest and poet Gonzalo de Berceo was one of the greatest followers of the mester de clerecía. All of his works were religious and two of the most well-known are *Milagros de Nuestra Señora* (about the miracles worked by the Virgin Mary) and *Vida de Santa Oria*. Fourteenth century poet Juan Ruíz, also known as the Arcipreste de Hita, used the cuadernia vía in parts of his famous work *Libro de buen amor*. He introduced sixteen syllable lines.

Spanish Prose

Spanish prose gained popularity in the mid-thirteenth century when King Alfonso X el Ṣabio of Castilla gave support and recognition to the writing form. He, with the help of his groups of intellectuals, directed the composition of many prose works including *Las siete partidas,* the first modern book of laws of the land written in the people's language. Another work was *La primera crónica general* which accounted for the history of Spain from the creation until the end of Alfonso's father's reign, San Fernando. It is the first national history ever written. For his direction of these works and many others he directed, Alfonso X is called the father of Spanish prose. His nephew, Don Juan Manuel is famous for his prose work *El Conde Lucanor* which is a frame story or short stories within an overall story. In this work, the Conde Lucanor seeks advice from his wise counselor, Patronio, who gives the advice through the telling of stories. Juan Manuel also wrote lesser-known works such as *El libro de los estados* on the social classes and *El libro del caballero y escudero* on philosophical discussions.

Toward the end of the Middle Ages, writer Fernando del Pulgar (1436-1490) created a new type of prose named the *verbal portrait.* This form is demonstrated by Pulgar's work *Claros varones de Castilla* in which he represents the detailed lives of twenty-four distinguished contemporaries. He explores their moral and psychological natures as well as physical traits. Pulgar was the official historian of the monarchs Fernando and Isabel, the famous Catholic Monarchs of Spain. This position gave him close encounters with the characters in this book, making the work realistic and detailed.

Lyric Poetry of the Middle Ages

Lyric poetry in the Middle Ages can be divided into three groups: the *jarchas,* the popular poems originating from folk-songs sung by commoners, and the courtly poetry of the nobles. Alfonso X el Sabio fits into the third group with his series of three hundred poems, written in Galician: *Las cantigas de Santa María.* Another poet, Juan Ruiz, or the Arcipreste de Hita is an outstanding lyricist of the fourteenth century. His only work, *Libro de buen amor* is a framework tale in which he includes translations from Ovid, satires, little poems called *serranillas,* twenty-nine fables, a sermon on Christian armor, and many lyric poems that praise the Virgin Mary. Poet *Íñigo López de Mendoza,* the Marqués de Santillana (1398-1458) begins to show the movement away from the traditions of the Middle Ages.

He shows a knowledge of Latin authors and familiarity with the works of Dante and Petrarch. Mendoza was also the first to introduce the sonnet into Spanish literature. The last great poet of the Middle Ages is Jorge Manrique. He is famous for his work which laments the death of his father, Coplas a la muerte de su padre. In this piece, Manrique shows classical feelings by expressing himself in a universal manner (all things come to an end). He is still considered a poet of the Middle Ages in that he finds peace and finality in religion.

Renaissance Literature

During the 15th century the pre-Renaissance occurs. Literary production increased exponentially. Some outstanding poets of this century are Juan de Mena and Íñigo López de Mendoza (Marquess of Santillana). The Spanish literature of the Middle Ages concludes with the work La Celestina by Fernando de Rojas.

In the Renaissance important topics are: the Renaissance poetry, with Garcilaso de la Vega and Juan Boscán; the religious literature, with Fray Luis de León, San Juan de la Cruz, and Santa Teresa de Jesús; and the Renaissance prosa, with the anonymous El Lazarillo de Tormes. The principal features of the Renaissance were the revival of learning based on classical sources, the rise of courtly patronage, the development of perspective in painting, and the advancements of science.

The most important characteristics of the Renaissance are:

- The language in this age is dominated by the naturality and simplicity, which avoids the affectation, the *amaneramiento* and the over-searched phrase. Thus the vocabulary and the syntax will be simple.
- The preferred themes are, fundamentally, love, conceived from the platonic point of view; nature, as somewhat idyllic (bucolic); pagan mythology, from which the histories of gods and the female beauty are reflected, following always the same classical ideal. In relation to these themes mentioned, various Renaissance points exist, some of them taken from the classical world:

— The *Carpe Diem*, whose translation would be "seize the day" or "take advantage of the moment". It advises the enjoyment of the life before the arrival of old age.

— The female beauty, described always following the same plan: blond youth, of serene, clear eyes, of white skin, red lips, rosy cheeks, etc.

— The *Beatus Ille* or praise of the life in the field, apart from the material things, as opposed to the life in the city, with its dangers and intrigues.

— The *Locus Emoenus* or description of a perfect and idyllic nature.

10

Medieval Theatre

Medieval theatre refers to the theatre of Europe between the fall of the Western Roman Empire and the beginning of the Renaissance. The term refers to a variety of genres because the time period covers approximately a thousand years of the art form and an entire continent. Most medieval theatre is not well documented due to a lack of surviving records and texts, a low literacy rate of the general population, and the opposition of the clergy to some types of performance.

At the beginning of the Middle Ages, the Roman Catholic Church banned theatrical performances, mostly as an attempt to curb the excesses of the Roman theatre. The Roman theatre was in decline because the economic and political conditions could not support the vast entertainment industry that had grown up in the empire and included circuses, horse races, gladiatorial combat, and the Roman comedies that are still sometimes performed today.

Very little is known about secular drama during the early medieval time. However, the anonymous pagan play "Querolus", written c.420, was adapted in the 12th century by Vitalis of Blois. Other secular Latin plays were also written in the 12th century, mainly in France but also in England ("Babio"). There certainly existed some other performances that were not fully fledged theatre; they may have been carryovers from the original pagan cultures (as is known from records written by the clergy disapproving of such festivals). It is also known that mimes, minstrels, bards, storytellers, and jugglers traveled in search of new audiences and financial support. Not much is known about these performers' repertoire and few written texts survive. One of the most famous of the secular plays is the musical "Le Jeu de Robin et Marion", written by Adam de la Halle in the 13th century, which is fully laid out in the original manuscript with lines, musical notation, and illuminations in the margins depicting the actors in motion. Adam also wrote another secular play, "Jeu de la Fueillee" in Arras, a French town in which theatre was thriving in the late 12th and 13th centuries. Perhaps the finest play surviving from Arras, is the "Jeu de saint Nicolas" by Jean Bodel.

Development of Medieval Drama

The Greeks, from the rudest beginnings, and by the aid of their incomparable instinct for form, brought to perfection a lofty type of tragedy and an original kind of comedy. The Latins, who had at least the germ of a comic drama of their own, were proud to borrow the comedy of the Greeks, although in their hands it could not but be sadly sterile. In the stalwart days of the Roman commonwealth the drama seems to have had scant encouragement in the capital, either from the men of culture or from the coarser populace. When at last the empire solidified itself upon the ruins of the republic, and the eagles of Rome were borne almost to the confines of the world, the cosmopolitan inhabitants of this immense realm were never educated to appreciate the calm pleasures of theater. They were encouraged to prefer the fierce joy of the chariot-race, the brutal delight of the arena, and the poignant ecstasy of gladiatorial combat. The sole vestiges of the true drama were the vulgar farces of the rustics that lingered in odd corners of Italy, and the obscene and cruel pantomimes which were devised to gratify the relish of the mob for lewdness and to glut its liking for gore. Neither the rough comic plays of the peasants nor the abominable pantomimes of the court had any relation to literature.

After the conversion of Constantine, the lustful and bloody spectacles were accurst by the church. It was to be expected that the Fathers should condemn the theater absolutely, since it was—in the sole aspect in which they had occasion to behold it—unspeakably vile. With the triumph of Christianity theatrical performances were abolished; and it must have seemed as though the drama was destroyed forever. It is true that in some obscure nooks rural farces might linger, forgotten links in the chain that was to stretch from the Atellan fables to the late Italian comedy-of-masks. But this doubtful survival seems to have little significance, and apparently the break in the tradition of the theater was final and irreparable. When Constantinople supplanted Rome as the capital of civilization, dramatic literature, which had been a chief glory of Athens, ceased from off the earth. For a thousand years and more the history of the drama is all darkness and vacancy; and we have not a single name recorded of any author writing plays to be performed by actors, in a theater, before an audience.

The desire for the drama, which seems to be instinctive in human nature the wide world over, from the Aleutian Islanders to the Bushmen of Australia, the impulse to personate and to take pleasure in beholding a story set forth in action,—this may have been dormant during the long centuries, or it may have found some means of gratifying itself unrecorded in the correspondence of the time or by the chroniclers. Acrobats there were, and wandering minstrels; and now and again we catch glimpses of singers of comic songs and of roving amusers who entertained with feats of sleight-of-hand, or who exhibited trained animals. These performers, always popular with the public at large, were also called in upon occasion to enliven the solid feasts of the rulers. Gibbon records that at the supper-table of Theodoric, in the middle of the fifth century, buffoons and performers of pantomimes were "sometimes introduced to divert, not do offend, the company by their ridiculous wit." And Froissart records that when he was a guest at the court of Gaston Phébus, toward the end of the fourteenth century, strolling jesters sometimes presented a little play during the repast, or acrobats went through their daring performances. The entertainments described by Gibbons and by Froissart, however long the interval between them, bear an obvious likeness to our latter-day "vaudevill suppers."

But none the less dramatic literature, which had flourished so gloriously in Greece, and which had tried to establish itself in Italy, was dead at last; and even the memory of it seems to have departed, for, in so far as the works of the Attic tragedians and of the Roman comedians were known at all, they were thought of rather as poetry to be read than as plays that had been acted. The art of acting was a lost art, and the theaters themselves fell into ruin. So it was that when the prejudice against the drama wore itself out in time, and when the inherent demand for the pleasure which only the theater can give became at last insistent, there was to be seen the spontaneous evolution of a new form, fitted specially to satisfy the needs of the people under the new circumstances. This new drama of the middle ages sprang into being wholly uninfluenced by the drama of the Greeks; it was, indeed, as free a growth as the Attic drama itself had been.

In its origin again, the medieval drama was not unlike the drama of the Greeks,—in that the germ or it was religious, and that it was slowly elaborated from what was at first only a casual accompaniment of public worship. The new form had its birth actually at the base of the altar and at the foot of the pulpit; and it was fostered by the Christian church, the very organization that had cursed the old form when that was decadent and corrupted. Coming into being as an illustrative incident of the service on certain special days of the ecclesiastical year, the drama grew sturdily within the walls of the church until it was strong enough to support itself; and when at last it ventured outside, it remained for a long while religious in intent. The history of its development is very much the same throughout Europe; and the religious drama of England is very like that of France (from which, indeed, it is in some measure derived), just as the religious drama of Italy is like that of Spain, although neither of these had any appreciable influence on the other.

The reason for this uniformity is obvious enough. It was due to the double unity of the medieval world,—that which resulted from possession of the same religion and that which was caused by the consciousness of a former union under the rule of Rome. All the peoples of western Europe had inherited the same customs and the same traditions, because they had all been included in the Roman Empire, which had stretched itself from the Black Sea to the Atlantic. When, at last, the vigor of the Roman government was relaxed, the barbarians of the north had broken in and had swept through southern Europe into Africa and into Asia. The Franks had taken Gaul for their own, the Goths had repopulated Italy, and the Vandals had traversed Spain; and as they had all of them accepted Christianity, sooner or later, the most distant lands had once more come under the sway of Rome.

This is why it is that we find in the middle ages a unity of western and southern Europe closer than ever before or ever since. Just before the Renaissance, the peoples of these varied stocks, however much they might differ individually, were bound together by the common use of the Latin language and by the common dominion of the Roman law; they held the same beliefs and they yielded to the same superstitions; they revered the same ideals, they acted on the same theories, and they had very much the same habits. As yet the idea of nationality had not been born; and the solidarity of those speaking each of the modern languages had not been suggested. Europe was a unit because, although it was segregated into towns and even into small provinces, these had not yet been compacted into distinct nations. Towns and provinces and kingdoms were all in accord in accepting the supremacy of the pontiff of Rome and in yielding a doubtful allegiance to the head of the shadowy monarchy which was still called the Holy Roman Empire.

To declare with certainty just where it was that the new drama first gave sign of life is quite impossible; and it is equally impossible to decide whether it sprang up of its own accord in half a dozen different places, or whether the first tempting suggestion of it was carried abroad in churches widely scattered. There was far more migration in the middle ages than is admitted by those who consider them merely as a long period of stagnation. Priests and merchants were continually passing from one city to another a thousand miles distant; and as the most of Europe was included in the Holy Roman Empire, and as it acknowledged also the sway of the Roman Pope, men could remove from the east to the west, and from the south to the north, with no feeling that they were relinquishing their nationality, especially as the priests, at least, could make themselves understood everywhere in the same tongue.

Latin was the language of the church and of its liturgy; and it is out of the Latin liturgy of the Christian church that the drama of the modern European languages has been slowly developed. It is not possible to trace all the steps by which a very brief semi-dramatic adjunct of the service of certain special days of the ecclesiastical year was slowly elaborated into a more or less complete dramatic scene; and it is difficult to declare just how it was that these several scenes were in time detached from the liturgy and combined together in a cycle which represented the chief events of the gospel-story. But it is practicable to prove that there was a steady growth, beginning with a single brief scene acted within the church, by the priests, in Latin, and almost as part of the liturgy, and developing, in the course of time, into a sequence of scenes, acted by laymen outside the church, in the vernacular, and wholly disconnected from the service.

The Christian church had so arranged its calendar that every one of the chief events in the career of Jesus was regularly commemorated in the course of the year. Its liturgy was rich in symbolism; and as the ritual was not everywhere uniform, opportunities were frequent for suggestive variations devised by the devout priests, who were diligently seeking the means by which they could best bring home the central truths of religion to a very ignorant congregation. In many churches, for example, the crucifix was removed from the altar on Good Friday and borne to a receptacle supposed to represent the sepulcher, whence it was taken on Easter morning to be restored solemnly to the altar, in testimony of the Resurrection.

The gospel-story is rarely pure narrative; as it is to be expected in the accounts of eye-witnesses, it abounds in actual dialogue. And where a dramatic passage was included in the service nothing was easier or more natural than to let the narrative be read by the officiating priest, while assigning the actual dialogue to other priests, each of whom should deliver the speeches of a single character. Thus on Easter morning, in the colloquy between Saints Peter and John and the three Marys, when the apostles ask what had been seen at the sepulcher, each of the three Marys can answer in turn. In time this interchange of dialogue would lend itself to amplification; and there is preserved a Latin manuscript in which the scene at the sepulcher was presented both in dialogue and in action. In this interpolation into the Easter service, the three Marys, Saint Peter and Saint John, and "One in the likeness of a gardener," all impersonated by priests or choirboys, speak the words set down for them in the sacred text, and do whatever is there recorded for them.

Although scenes of this sort seem to have been first invented to imbellish the Easter services, Christmas was soon discovered to offer an equal opportunity. For example, one of the very earliest of these enlargements of the ritual showed the quest of the shepherds. At the proper moment certain priests holding crooks in their hands are to be seen standing in the transept, and a chorister from a gallery above announces to them the glad tidings of the birth of Christ, the Savior of men. Then, while other choristers scattered throughout the galleries sing, "Glory to God in the highest, and on earth peace, good will to men," the Shepherds advance to the choir, and halt at length before a manger which has been arranged near the altar and by the side of an image of the Virgin Mary. There two other priests, personating Women who had aided the Virgin-mother, ask the Shepherds what it is they are seeking, and then display the infant Jesus to them. The Shepherds, after adoring the new-born babe and its mother, depart singing "For unto us a child is born,"—which is the beginning of the high mass regularly celebrated at Christmas.

More elaborate is a liturgical embellishment dealing with the Three Kings, the Three Wise Men of the East, and calling for a greater variety of characters and for a more obvious effort to indicate the different localities where the several portions of the gospel story were supposed to take place. The huge churches, which had begun to spring up all over Europe in the century following the fateful year 1000, were not encumbered with pews, as are our smaller modern edifices; and their free floor-space would contain multitudes of spectators, even though lanes were kept open through the throng to connect the altar and the various doors. Within the chancel was the manger, with an image of the Virgin-mother; and also two priests stood there, personating Women who had been assisting Mary.

In a pulpit, or in a gallery, was the chorister who was to sing the message of the Angel. On a platform not far distant was a throne, on which Herod sat, surrounded by the members of his court, all of these characters being assumed by officials of the church. The Angel, the two Women by the manger, and Herod and his courtiers, were each in their several stations in the church before the play began; and they were supposed not to be able to see one another,--indeed, they were supposed not even to be present until it should be the turn of each to enter into the action.

First the Shepherds come into the church by one of the doors; and, passing through the ranks of the congregation, they advance toward the choir, where the Angel hails them with the glad tidings, whereupon they go to the manger and adore the holy babe; and at last, after singing, they stand apart. Then through another door on the eastern side of the church enter the Three Kings; and when they have come to the middle of the edifice a star begins to guide them to the manger,—this star being a light pulled along a wire. Herod, silent on his throne all this time, has been supposed not to see the Shepherds; but the Kings he does see, and so he sends a Messenger to ask who they are. The Messenger questions them at length, and finally bears back to Herod the dread news that the King of Kings has been born, and that the Three Wise Men of the East are being guided to his cradle by the star above their heads. Herod then consults the Scribes, who proceed to search the Scriptures and to inform him that the promised Redeemer should be born in Bethlehem. Herod rages violently at these ill-tidings, and knocks the books from the hands of the Scribes; but, pacified by his son, he bids the Three Wise Men follow the star and find the newborn King, commanding them on their return to let him know where the royal infant lay.

Herod and all his courtiers then become silent again, and cease to take part in the play until they shall be once more needed. The Three Kings, bearing their gifts and led by the star, advance toward the altar and meet the Shepherds, who now come into the action again. The Shepherds sing a hymn of praise; and the Three Kings ask them what they have seen. The Shepherds, after declaring that they have beheld the holy child lying in a manger, withdraw; and the Three Kings follow the star to the alter, where the two Women ask them who they are and what they are seeking.

The Three Wise Men reveal the object of their journeying; and the babe is then displayed to them. They adore it, presenting their gifts of gold and frankincense and myrrh. The Angel in the pulpit or gallery above them breaks in, declaring that the prophecies are fulfilled, and bidding the Three Kings go home by another way. Thereupon the Wise Men, chanting a hymn of praise, pass through the assembled multitude and leave the church by a western door. Herod is supposed not to have seen them take their leave, but just as soon as they are gone, the Messenger informs the monarch that they have departed in disobedience; thereupon Herod draws his sword and gives it to a Soldier, bidding him go forth and slay all the children.

Here the play seems to end, although, as we have also the manuscript of a representation of the Flight into Egypt and of the Slaughter of the Innocents, it is probable that, in some churches, on some occasions, all the various incidents connected with the Nativity were set forth in action, one after the other. What it is most important for us to seize and to fix in our memories is that these episodes of the gospel-story—the Scene of the Shepherds, the Adoration of the Wise Men, the Wrath of Herod, the Slaughter of the Innocents—came into existence each by itself, having been put into dramatic form as a more vivid and impressive illustration of the liturgy; and that possibly a long while elapsed before any one thought to combine these scattered scenes into a sequence. But after the Christmas cycle of the Nativity had knit itself together, following or preceding a similar Easter cycle of the separate scenes of the Crucifixion and the Resurrection, it was probably not very long before an attempt was made to link the two cycles together, filling out the gaps by dramatizing the more interesting of the intervening episodes of the gospel-story,—the Raising of Lazarus, for instance, and the Driving of the Money-changers from the Temple. Thus the whole story of the life and death and resurrection of Jesus could be presented in dialogue in the church by the priests themselves, in Latin, and as part of the service, for the enlightenment of the ignorant population in those dark ages.

Although the priests who put it together had not given a thought to this aspect of it, the story of Jesus is truly dramatic, not only in its humanity, in its color, in its variety, in its infinite pathos, but also and chiefly in its full possession of the prime essential of a true drama—in its having at the heart of it a struggle, an exhibition of determination, a clash of contending desires. Indeed, it is the most dramatic of all struggles, for it is the perpetual conflict of good and evil. To us moderns the issue is sharply joined; but in the medieval church it was even more obvious, since in the middle ages no one ever doubted that a personal Devil was forever striving to thwart the will of a personal God. In the passion-play, which showed in action all the leading events of the life of Christ, both of the contestants were set boldly before the spectators—God himself high in Heaven, and the Devil escaping from Hell-mouth to work his evil will among mankind.

After all these little scenes, each of them devised originally for the special day of the church calendar when the event was commemorated, had been combined into a New Testament cycle, and after there had been prefixed to it certain episodes dramatized from the Old Testament also, and selected because they seemed to prefigure the gospel-story,—after the passion-play had become a mystery, and after it was thus grown to its full length and swollen huge, it was found to be too unwieldy for presentation in the church itself, and too burdensome for the clergy to perform. Thrust out of the church, it may have lingered for a while in the churchyard or in the cloisters or in the great square before the sacred edifice. As the successive episodes of the gospel-story no longer had an intimate connection with the actual liturgy, the tendency was increased to substitute for the Latin of the priests the language of the people; and this pressure became irresistible when the ecclesiastics gave up to laymen the acting of the several characters.

The performance of a full-grown mystery, with due regard to the dignity of the theme, was an undertaking of not a little magnitude, requiring both capital and executive ability. The preparation of the text, the adjusting of the music, the making ready of the costumes, the training of the actors,—these things were possible only to an organization of a certain stability. At first the church was the only body having at once the desire and the resources to execute so onerous a task. But when the guilds arose in time, and when burghers banded together and craftsmen combined, it became possible for the church to relinquish the control of the mysteries to lay organizations.

But although the evolution of the passion-play from the liturgy is obvious, we find in the mystery, when it was presented in the language of the people by the craftsmen and the burghers, one element which is not of ecclesiastical origin;—we find the element of humor, of joyous gaiety, of vivacious realism, and often indeed of reckless vulgarity. Even before it was wholly independent of the church the new drama had felt the influence of popular taste, and it had taken over more than one of the accepted devices of the primitive comic plays, such as the strolling buffoons were wont to perform. The brief farces of these wandering minstrels may have been mere dramatized anecdotes, practical jokes in dialogue, pantomimic horse-play of an elementary type; they were wholly unliterary, and being often even unwritten, they have rarely been preserved. Yet it is perfectly possible that this medieval farce, with its hearty fun and its frankness of speech, is the direct descendant of the rude humor of the Latin rustics, surviving unobserved and neglected through all the centuries of the dark ages, and serving humbly to satisfy, in some measure, the perpetual human desire for a story told in action. When at last the serious play had been developed out of the services of the church, this folk-drama was ready to supply the comic element, without which any representation of life muse needs be one-sided.

Fortunately chance has saved for our enlightenment not a few of the later specimens of this folk-play; and we can see that it was generally as unliterary and as inartistic as one might expect, and that it assumed a great variety of forms. It might be merely a burlesque-sermon satirizing the clergy or the civil authorities; it might be a monologue in which, for example, a boastful character unwillingly admitted his own unworthiness; it might be little more than a comic song with a telling refrain and with illustrative gestures; it might be a dialogue of cut-and-thrust repartee not unlike the pungent talk interchanged by the ringmaster and the clown in the modern circus; it might even be a lively little play with a simple ingenuity of situation, presenting a scene of every-day life with an abundance of pertinent detail.

Such, for example, is the French farce of the *TUB* with its three characters of the Husband, the Wife, and the Mother-in-law. The Husband is henpecked; and the Wife, aided by the Mother-in-law, has even gone so far as to draw up an agreement for the Husband to sign, in which he has bound himself to do all the work of the household, and in which his several duties are specified, item by item. Then, as it happens, the Wife falls into the tub in which they have been washing the household linen, and she cries to the husband to help her out. He consults the agreement, and then refuses to assist her, as that is not set down in writing. The Wife insists; and the Husband protests that he is willing to do all that he has agreed to do, but nothing more.

The Mother-in-law intervenes, but she cannot extricate the Wife without the Husband's help; and he refers her again to the document. He is ready to bake and to boil and to get up early to make the fire, as he has promised to do; but as for pulling the Wife out of the tub, that is not his duty, since it is not down in the bond. The Wife and the Mother-in-law scold and threaten at first; but at last they appeal. The Husband suggests that if he is to do more than he has bound himself to do in writing, then the agreement is really useless, and he proposes that it shall be torn up before he rescues the Wife. As her danger is now pressing, the two women agree to this; the bond is rent in twain, and the Husband extricates the Wife from the tub. The household is once more upon a peace footing; and yet the Husband, warned by experience, remarks to the spectators that he wonders how long it will last.

This little farce of *THE TUB* is French; but it has its analogs in the other modern literatures. It has a certain likeness to the dispute between Noah and his Wife in an English mystery—a very amusing scene, indeed, in which the spouse of the patriarch refuses to enter the ark unless she can bring her friends with her, and in which, when she is taken on board by force, she gives her venerable husband a sound box on the ear.

French, also, is the farce of *MASTER PETER PATELIN*, by far the most artistic of all the medieval comic plays. Patelin is a swindling lawyer who is in the depths of poverty. He goes to a Draper and wheedles him out of six yards of woolen cloth; and when the Draper comes to him for payment, Patelin is in bed, and his Wife protests that he has not been out of the house for weeks. The Draper is almost persuaded that he is the victim of hallucination, and he returns to the shop to see if he has truly lost his cloth. Finding that it is really gone, he rushes again to Patelin's lodging, whereupon the lawyer pretends to be mad, and overwhelms the unfortunate tradesman with a flood of words, first in one of the French dialects, and then in those of another, until at last the Draper withdraws, half believing that it is the devil who has played a trick on him. Then there comes to Patelin the Shepherd of the Draper, whom his master is suing for having stolen some sheep, and the Shepherd engages the lawyer to defend him.

Patelin bids the Shepherd to pretend to be foolish and no matter what question the Judge may put to him, to answer only with the bleat of a lamb,—"Baa-a!" When the trial comes before the Judge, Patelin hides himself behind the Shepherd so that the Draper shall not see him. But the shopkeeper does catch sight of the lawyer at last, and he instantly demands payment for his cloth, to the complete astonishment of the Judge, who had supposed that he was trying the Shepherd for sheep-stealing. The Draper gets confused also, and accuses the Shepherd of stealing the cloth and the lawyer of taking the sheep. The puzzled judge questions the Shepherd, who answers no word but "Baa-a!" and Patelin adroitly pleads that the poor fellow is plainly an idiot. The Draper continues to insist on payment for his cloth, although the judge in vain begs him to come back to his sheep. In the end, the magistrate has to acquit the Shepherd for lack of evidence against him. Then the wretched Draper asks Patelin if he is not the lawyer who had been seen in bed only a few minutes before; and Patelin daringly bids him go to the house and look for himself. When the tortured tradesman has departed, Patelin turns to the Shepherd and demands his fee for getting the man off from the charge against him. And now are the tables turned; for the Shepherd simply answers, "Baa-a!" The play comes to an end swiftly with the discomfited Patelin trying vainly to catch his deceitful client.

MASTER PETER PATELIN is a French farce, to be acted by itself whenever a company of strollers happened to have five performers; but it is curiously like one of the Nativity scenes in an English mystery. When the Shepherds are watching their flocks by night, a neighbor joins them—one Mak, a man of evil repute. To keep him under guard when they go to sleep, the Shepherds make Mak lie down between them. But the precaution is unavailing, as Mak gets up, and steals a lamb, and takes it to his Wife, and then returns to his place. When the Shepherds wake, there is Mak between them; but a lamb is missing. Mak is suspected at once, and the Shepherds go to his house, where Mak's Wife has the lamb swaddled in a cradle like a babe. The Shepherds search everywhere and find nothing, until one of them goes to the cradle and remarks that the babe has a long snout. When the lamb is discovered, Mak's Wife promptly pretends that it is a changeling just left by an elf. The Shepherds, after punishing Mak by tossing him in a blanket, return to their flock; and almost immediately the Angel above sings to them the glad tidings of Christmas morn. Here is a comic action, complete in itself and quite detachable from the mystery, with which, indeed, it has no necessary connection. Perhaps it is even older than the mystery, and was inserted into the text merely to supply what is known nowadays as "comic relief,"—just as the farce of *THE TUB* might have been incorporated into a passion-play without any protest from the public.

Both in French and in English the comic scenes of the mysteries were often wholly irrelevant in theme and absolutely incongruous in treatment. No reverence for the sacred subject prevented the medieval audience from enjoying a joke, or made it very particular as to the quality of the fun it laughed at. Just as we moderns are surprised by the grinning gargoyles and by the satiric carvings of the mighty cathedrals, so in the medieval drama we are often taken aback by the bold vulgarity of the comic scenes. Although the medieval writers had not found out that brevity is the soul of wit, they often acted on the belief that breadth is the body of humor.

The authors were plain of speech and the audiences were never squeamish; and as we study what was then to be seen on the stage we are reminded of Taine's remark that in the middle ages man lived on a dunghill. It must be noted that the farces are rather more reprehensible than the comic scenes of the mysteries; and yet the grossest of these farces might be performed sometimes as the prelude to a miracle-play; thus *THE MILLER* preceded a very devout dramatization of the legend of Saint Martin.

This low humor is indecorous rather than demoralizing; it shocks our sense of propriety sometimes, but it is never insidious or seductive. It was intended for the entertainment of the populace, which is often vulgar but which is rarely vicious. In the farces, as in the more serious scenes of the passion-plays, we can always see the simplicity and the sincerity which were ever the two chief characteristics of medieval endeavor.

THE change from the Latin language to the speech of the people, the transfer of control from the clergy to the laity, the removal from the inside of the church to the outside, were all made gradually and tentatively, and with no intent to bring about any radical transformation. When the laymen took charge, they desired to do just what the priests had done, no more and no less; and if we seek to understand the circumstances of the performances outside the church, we must recall what the conditions were originally inside the sacred edifice. In the cycle of the Nativity we saw that the manger was set up near the altar, and that not far distant there was erected a throne for Herod. Each of these places was thus what came to be known as a "station"; and the action of the play went on, not only at the one or the other of the stations, but also in other parts of the church, extending now and again even to the doors.

The Easter cycle would also require several stations,—three at least, one with a throne for Pilate, another with the cross, a third with the open grave. The acting of the play was carried on chiefly in the open space between and in front of the several stations, the characters belonging to each of these remaining there, silent and motionless, until the time came for them to enter with the story. Then they might leave the station for a while, and go out into the open space, only to return to their own places so soon as the progress of the plot called for the characters of some other station.

When the Christmas cycle and the Easter cycle were combined together, and when the few intermediate scenes were also cast into dialogue, so that the whole earthly life of Jesus might be shown, from his birth to his resurrection, then the nave of the church would be inconveniently crowded with the many stations requisite for the whole gospel-story; and there would be left between them, and in front, an inadequate area for what might be termed the neutral ground, the open space for the acting of the many scenes which did not call for special stations—such, for instance, as the Entry into Jerusalem, or the Betrayal at Gethsemane. Those who began to act out the sacred story in the church had no thought of scenery,—which, indeed, was a thing to them not only unknown, but wholly inconceivable.

They were seeking to show what had happened on the very day they were commemorating. Even when the incidents had cohered into a sequence, it was the action itself that was all important, and the place where it came to pass was without significance except when it needed to be specified. So the most of the acting was always in the more open space in the center; and stations were utilized only when they were really necessary. Probably as the mysteries increased in length the number of necessary stations became cumbersome, and only in the larger cathedrals would it be possible to avoid an awkward cluttering within the chancel. Quite possibly, this multiplication was an added reason for removing the performance of the mysteries outside the church, so some ampler place, where the several stations might be more widely separated.

When this removal did take place, and the mysteries were presented in the open air, what the laymen who took charge of them would undoubtedly seek to do would be to preserve carefully such traditions as had been established in the course of the performances given by the clergy. These laymen would therefore avail themselves of the device of the stations, modifying these as might be required by the new conditions of performance. In England this modification came in time to be somewhat different from that obtaining in France; but as the English mystery is derived from French models, the French form demands attention first, the more so as elsewhere in Europe there is a closer resemblance to French usage than to English.

In France, then, a mystery would be acted upon a platform put up in some public place, often in the open square in front of the cathedral. To provide reserved seats for the dignitaries of the church, the officials of the city, and the distinguished strangers invited to attend, grandstands would be erected facing the platform and along the sides, the central area being left free for the populace, who were always eager to crowd in, while the gaily draped windows of the surrounding houses would be available as private boxes. The platform, intended to serve as a stage, was perhaps a hundred and fifty feet long, and some fifty or sixty feet deep. The front part was generally free and clear, so that the actors could move to and fro, while at the back were ranged the stations—which in

France came soon to be known as "mansions." At the extreme left of the spectators, and raised high on pillars, was Heaven, wherein God sat, often with a gilded face, the better to suggest the shining glory of his countenance. At the extreme right of the spectators was Hell-mouth, the fiery cavern where the Devil and all his imps had their abode. Then stretching from Heaven to Hell-mouth was the line of mansions, those earliest in use being on the left. A wall, pierced by a door, might indicate Nazareth; next an altar covered by a canopy and protected by a balustrade would suggest the Temple; and a second wall with its gate could serve to call up the idea of Jerusalem itself. In the center there might be a more elaborate construction, with columns and a throne, intended for the palace of Pontius Pilate. A third wall with two doors might be made to serve as the house of the high-priest and as the Golden Gate; while in front of this and not far from Hell-mouth there might be a tank of real water, with a little boat floating on it, so as to simulate the Sea of Gennesaret.

These are the mansions that are depicted in a miniature on the manuscript of a mystery acted in Valenciennes in the middle of the sixteenth century. In other places, and at other times, there might be more or there might be less, for there was never any uniformity of custom; and even here we see that many of the most important episodes of the gospel-narrative must have been performed on the front part of the platform and wholly unrelated to any of the mansions ranged at the back. The mansions were employed only when certain portions of the sacred story could, by their use, be made clearer or more striking; and even when they were set up, however elaborate their decoration might be, it was never in any way deceptive. The mansions were not intended actually to represent the special places; the most they were expected to do was to suggest them so that a few columns would indicate a palace or a temple, and so that a wall and a door sufficed to evoke the idea of a city.

Thus we see that in France the stations used inside the church were set up side by side on the open-air stage outside of the church, where they were known as mansions. In England, when the passion-play was taken out of the sacred edifice, another arrangement was adopted: the stations were separated and each was shown by itself, being called a "pageant." Sometimes these were immovable, and sometimes they were ambulatory; and in the latter case, which seems to have been the more frequent, the pageant was apparently not unlike the elaborately decorated "floats" familiar in modern parades, such as that of Mardi Gras in New Orleans.

Corpus Christi day was early chosen as the festival most fit for the performance of the mysteries; and in Great Britain the pageants followed in the wake of the Corpus Christi procession through the town. The first pageant, with its appropriate decorations and its own groups of performers, would draw up before the church-door as the end of the procession emerged therefrom; and the first episode of the play would then be represented there, sometimes on the broad platform of the wagon, but often in the street itself,—just as most of the acting in the French mysteries took place not so much in the mansions themselves as in the neutral ground in front of the stage. One stage-direction in an English manuscript is curiously significant: "Here Herod shall rage on the pageant and in the street."

When the first episode had been played out, the second pageant appeared; and the first pageant was dragged away along the line of march of the Corpus Christi procession to another appointed spot, where the first episode was acted again, while the performers attached to the second pageant were presenting the second episode before the doors of the church. Then a third pageant would take the place of the second; and thus it was that, in the course of the long summer day, the spectator, no matter at which of the chosen spots he might chance to stand, could see all the successive incidents of the mystery represented before him, partly on the pageants, with their elementary attempts to indicate the actual place where the action was supposed to be passing, and partly in the open street in the space that was kept clear for the actors. For certain of the episodes, such as the Trial of Jesus, for example, two pageants were necessary, and the performers passed from one to the other as the incidents of the narrative might require.

This use of ambulatory pageants seems to have obtained chiefly in the English towns; and in the rural districts the pageants were not decorated wagons, but platforms set up along the route of the Corpus Christi procession. There was a stage for each of the important episodes of the play, thus recalling the original stations devised for the performance when it took place inside the church. The spectators, following the procession, would halt in front of the first platform and witness the acting of the first episode; and when that was concluded they would pass along to the second platform to behold the second episode; and so on until they had seen the entire mystery. The English were thus setting up separately the stations which the French had preferred to put side by side upon one very long platform. But these variations of custom between the French and the English are external only, and of no immediate importance, although they account in part for the divergence to be observed in the development of the later dramatic literatures of the two languages.

Essentially the mystery is the same, wherever it is acted, and in whatever language, French or English, German or Italian. It is the same in its long-windedness and in its loose-jointedness, in its homely directness of speech alternating with turgid bombast, in its occasional touches of genuine feeling and of unrestrained pathos, in the introduction of humorous scenes, in the frank realism of the dialogue, and, above all, in the simple faith of those who wrote it, of those who acted it, and of those who beheld its performance. The influence of the audience must always be taken into account: and the medieval spectators for whose edification the mystery was devised were unlearned and without culture; they were ignorant and even gross; they had no tincture of letters; they were credulous and superstitious and wonder-loving; they were at once devout and irreverent,—or at least they seem so to us; they had a liking for broad fun and for a robust realism of treatment; they were shocked by no vulgarity and they resented incongruity, for they were wholly devoid of the historic sense.

Although the English mysteries were of Anglo-Norman origin and follow the French tradition in the main, yet the bond of unity was broken when Latin was abandoned for the vernacular; and there are other differences between the performances in French and those in English besides the modification of the station into the mansion in the one country and into the pageant in the other. In England, the entire mystery—shortened now and again by the occasional omission of one episode or another—seems sometimes to have been presented in a single day, the exhibition beginning as early as four in the morning. In France the performance was more likely to continue over several successive days, very much as the Wagnerian cycle is now given at Bayreuth,—although it may be doubted whether any modern audience could have the patience of the medieval spectators of Bourges who in the sixteenth century were entertained by a mystery of the *ACTS OF THE APOSTLES*, the performance of which took forty days.

In England, as we have seen, the pageants followed the religious procession; whereas in France, where the mansions were immovable on a single platform, it was not unusual for the whole troop of performers to make a street-parade before the acting began, quite in the manner of the modern travelling circus. In France, again, when the church gave up control of the mysteries, they were turned over to lay organizations of burghers, founded especially to perform the sacred plays; whereas in England this task was assumed by the gilds, each of which undertook the episode which its craftsmanship best fitted it to carry out, the Carpenters, for instance, being responsible for Noah's Ark, and the Goldsmiths undertaking the Three Kings, because they could best provide the royal diadems.

Further differences there are also between the mysteries as performed in France or in England and the sacred-representations of the Italians; and again between the dramatizations of the Scriptures as acted in Germany and those to be seen in Spain. But these differences are matters of detail merely; and the line of development was everywhere the same throughout those parts of Europe that had been ruled by Rome. Everywhere also was the production of a mystery considered as a good deed, as an act pleasing to Heaven, and certain to win favor from the Deity and from the saints.

Such performances were often, therefore, given in a season or pestilence to placate the wrath of God or to deserve the protection of some particular saint. Such an exhibition took place in Constantinople, within Saint Sophia itself, in the middle of the fifteenth century, just before the capture of the capital of the Western Empire by the Turks. Mysteries were also performed in certain towns after an escape from impending danger and as a testimony of gratitude to Heaven for its intervention; and it is to this sentiment that we owe the continued performance of the passion-play, which is still to be seen every tenth summer at Oberammergau.

The majority of the mysteries preserved to us in manuscript are anonymous, and of only a few are we acquainted with the exact date of composition. Most of the authors are to be considered rather as compilers; lacking individuality, they were satisfied to accept the play as they found it, modifying the framework but little after it had once been constructed, and satisfying themselves with adding or subtracting episodes at will. Each of them freely availed himself of the labors of those of his predessors with which he chanced to be familiar. Sometimes he rewrote what he borrowed, and sometimes he copied it slavishly, careless of any diversity of diction. So there is not often harmony of style in any single mystery; and yet there is an immense monotony when a number of them are compared together.

VERY closely allied to the mystery was the miracle-play, which may have come into being even before the Easter cycle had elaborated itself intoa passion-play. A sequence of episodes taken from Holy Writ we now call a mystery; and what we now call a miracle-play is a sequence of episodes taken from the life of some wonder-working saint. In England the mystery was much the more frequent; but in France the miracle-play was perhaps the more popular, as it was probably almost as ancient. Indeed, in the middle ages no one seems ever to have made any distinction between the two kinds of play, as the medieval mind was not trained to discriminate between the canonical books and the Apocrypha, or even between the Scriptures and the legends of the saints. In miracle-play, as in mystery, we find the same naïve treatment of life, the same panoramic construction of the story, the same admixture of comic incidents, and the same apparent irreverence; and the circumstances of the performance would be the same also.

The middle ages had an appetite for allegory quite as vigorous as the liking for legend; and after the saintly biographies had been set on the stage as miracle-plays, allegory was also cast into dialogue, and thus we have the moral-plays. The morality was a medieval forerunner of our modern novel-with-a-purpose, as unconvincingly didactic as it is inevitably dull. The morality may even be defined as an attempt to dramatize a sermon,—whereas the mystery is simply a dramatization of the text. Written to be presented before an audience used to the primitive methods of the passion-play, the authors make free use of the device of the stations, for instance. In one morality, the *CASTLE OF CONSTANCY*, there were six stations: one was a castellated structure open below to reveal a bed for the chief character, who personified the Human Race; and the other five stations were disposed around this loftier stage, one in the east for God, one in the northeast for Greed, one in the west for the World, one in the south for the Flesh, and one in the north for the Devil.

The hero of this string of argumentative conversations, Human Race, appears at first as a child, and the Angels of Good and of Evil come to him. He is tempted off to the World by the Evil Angel; and later, as a young man, he is introduced to the Seven Deadly Sins. In time Repentance leads him to Confession; and as a man of forty we see him in the Castle of Constancy, surrounded by the Seven Most Excellent Virtues. Thereupon the Castle itself is besieged by three evil powers and the Seven Deadly Sins and their allies. Then at last, as an old man, Human Race backslides again, and the Evil Angel is bearing him away, when a formal trial takes place before God, at which Justice and Truth accuse him, while he is defended by Mercy and Peace.

The morality was an attempt to depict character, but with the aid of violent colors only, and with a harsh juxtaposition of light and darkness. Yet it helped along the development of the drama in that it permitted a freer handling of the action, since the writer of moralities had always to invent his plots, whereas the maker of mysteries had his stories ready-made to his hand. The morality was frankly fiction, while the miracle-play gave itself out for fact. Then, also, the tendency seems irresistible for an author who has any appreciation of human nature to go speedily from the abstract to the concrete and to substitute for the cold figure of Pride itself the less frigid portrait of an actual man who is proud. Thus mere allegory, barren and chill, is swiftly warmed into social satire, tingling with individuality; and so we have here before us the germ out of which a living comedy was to be evolved. It is to be noted that when the morality had achieved a certain freedom for itself in plot and in character, it seems to have exerted a healthy influence upon the contemporary mystery and miracle-play.

In fact, the medieval mind did not distinguish the three kinds of drama sharply, and we find them commingled in more than one example,—notably in the English *MARY MAGDALENE.* We discover the same confusion of species in all uncritical periods, when production is spontaneous and unconscious. In method the mystery and the miracle-play are alike; and by no certain mark can we set off the morality from the interlude in English or the monologue from the burlesque-sermon in French. The more elevated the effort, the more likely was an admixture of the grotesque. Immediately before or after the loftiest moments of a tragic theme, the nimble devils would come capering forth to make the spectator shriek with laughter at their buffoonery as they bore away some evil-doer to be cast into Hell-mouth.

Popular as these plays were, it is only in a chance episode that any one of them is really raised into literature. The drama must be the most democratic of all the arts, since its very existence depends on the multitude; and it is therefore likely always to represent the average intelligence of any era. The long period known as the middle ages, whatever its literary unattractiveness, brought about a new birth of the acted drama. It aroused in the people the desire for the pleasures of the theater; and it began to train actors against the time when acting should once more become a profession.

In considering the deficiencies of the medieval drama, we must never forget that the actors were all amateurs,—priests at first, and then burghers and craftsmen, students and clerks. They might be paid for their services, or they might choose to perform as a labor of love; but acting was not their calling, and their opportunities for improving themselves in the art were infrequent. The accomplished actor stimulates the dramatist, and the playwright is ever developing the performer; each is necessary to the other, and in the middle ages we find neither. Yet slowly the traditions of a theater were getting themselves established.

There was acting, such as it was; there were plays, such as they were, not so much dramas as mere panoramas of successive episodes; there were audiences, rude and gross, no doubt, but composed of human beings, after all, and therefore ever ready to be entranced and thrilled by the art of the master-craftsman. But in the medieval drama we seek in vain for a master-craftsman; he is not to be found in France or in England, in Spain, in Italy, or in Germany. The elements of a vital drama were all there, ready to the hand of a true dramatist who might know how to make use of them; they were awaiting the grasp of a poet-playwright who might be able to present with technical skill and with imaginative insight the perpetual struggle of good and evil, of God and the Devil.

But in all medieval literature there is no born playwright; and there is no born poet who wrought in dialogue and action. The one indestructible work of art which gives utterance to the intentions of the middle ages, to the ideals of that dark time, and to its aspirations, was not made to be represented within the church or out of it, either by priests or by laymen, even though it bore the name of the DIVINE COMEDY.

Staging

Depending upon the location of the performances, the plays were performed either in inn yards, on pageant wagons in the streets of great cities, in the halls of knights, on top of a mountain and lords, or apparently in the round in amphitheatres, suggested by current archaeology in Cornwall and the southwest of England. These latter stages are often called "Place and Scaffold", or "Locus and Platea" and were not purpose built for the theater, but a general purpose outdoor location also used for activities such as ball games or bull baiting. Therefore, all stage production was temporary and expected to be removed upon the completion of the performances. The Locus, or Place, was the open field or amphitheatre ground where much of the general action took place. The Scaffolds, or Platea, sometimes also called Mansions or Houses, were small stages often built up on a raised scaffold to represent specific kinds of locations such as a castle or Heaven. The actors were expected to travel between these Houses in order to enact scene changes, rather than remain stationary and have the scene change around them as is typically done in modern theater.

Decline and Change

Its death was due mostly to changing political and economic factors. First, the Protestant Reformation targeted the theatre, especially in England, in an effort to stamp out allegiance to Rome. In Wakefield, for example, the local mystery cycle text shows signs of Protestant editing, with references to the pope crossed out and two plays completely eliminated because they were too Catholic. However, it was not just the Protestants who attacked the theatre of the time. The Council of Trent banned religious plays in an attempt to rein in the extrabiblical material that the Protestants frequently lampooned.

A revival of interest in ancient Roman and Greek culture changed the tastes of the learned classes in the performing arts. Greek and Roman plays were performed and new plays were written that were heavily influenced by the classical style. This led to the creation of Commedia dell'arte and other forms of Renaissance theatre.

A change of patronage also caused drastic changes to the theatre. In England the monarch and nobility started to support professional theatre troupes (including Shakespeare's Lord Chamberlas Men and King's Men), which catered to their upper class patron's tastes. These patrons desired to be entertained, not preached to, and as time passed the plays became more secular and refined. In time these same tastes would filter down to the lower classes.

Finally, the construction of permanent theaters, such as the Blackfriars Theatre signaled a major turning point from reliance on church facilities, touring groups, and inns as stages. Permanent theaters allowed for more sophisticated staging and storytelling. Moreover, professional troupes that owned their own theatre had more resources with which to prepare their productions, which changed the theatre from a mostly amateur or traveling art form to a professional one with different practices and standards.

Genres

Mummings are one of the earliest styles of Medieval drama. Early as it was, it still had very strong pagan roots, with appearances of St. Nick right alongside the Green Man, a pagan vegetation god. While these plays were performed in yearly rituals, such as the summer and winter solstices and spring and summer equinoxes, the most important remains as the Yule Mummings. These performances were public communal processions in common social areas, excepting chapels. Mummings were also unapologetically politically incorrect.

Mysteries, or "Cycle" plays, were performed in each summer. These plays were a joint effort by the community, in which different guilds were assigned a portion of the Bible to act out on a makeshift stage—wagons—in a community square. For instance, the blacksmith guild, makers of nails, would perform the Crucifixion of Christ. As is tradition, only man acted on the stage in the Medieval period. However, women are allowed and expected to act in England's modern renditions. These plays were utterly didactic and deeply scriptural, focused on sharing the gospel story. The most famous of these is the Wakefield Master's Second Shepherd's Play.

Miracle Plays widened its religious horisons and focused on spirituality outside of the Bible, instead dramatising the lives of canonised Saints. The heavy emphasis on absolute Truth instead of fact meant that events in the plays may not have been realistic.

Morality plays were heavily allegorical and straight didacticism, instructing man in what he should do. These can be extremely entertaining. The great focus of the morality play is death. In a post-plague Europe, death was considered a great equaliser because everyone goes with death eventually. The most famous of the Morality plays is Everyman, originally a Dutch play. In this, a character named Everyman is beckoned by Death, and seeks the aid of other personified elements, such as Good Deeds and Kinsmen, before ultimately following Death.

In the very late Medieval period, bridging this age with the Renaissance, Manners Plays came out. These plays focused on the social and secular instead of the religious, taking the idea of the morality play and putting it in a social world instead of a spiritual. Often, the plays depict people acting socially inappropriately.

1) *Quem Quaeritis*—the piece of the liturgical Easter mass that eventually grew into a huge body of religious drama
2) "The Second Shepherds' Play" from the Wakefield (also called Towneley) Cycle
3) The York cycle—the longest mystery cycle in existence
4) *Everyman*--this Flemish play is the most famous morality play
5) *The Castle of Perseverance*—from 1440, a full-length vernacular play. It's especially important because a stage drawing is included, which may suggest theatre in the round.

6) "La Farce de maître Pierre Pathelin"—A French farce that was very popular for over a century.

7) *Le Jeu de Robin et Marion*— complete 13th century French pastoral musical comedy.

Most authors of medieval plays are anonymous. Important ones are:

1) Hrosvitha—the first female playwright, a nun from Gandersheim

2) The Wakefield Maste—contributor to some of the plays of the Wakefield Cycle, including "The Second Shepherds' Play." His real name is not known.

3) John Bale—English churchman

4) Adam de la Halle—French composer

Bibliography

Anderson, Graham (2004), *King Arthur in Antiquity*, London: Routledge.

Barber, Richard (1986), *King Arthur: Hero and Legend*, Woodbridge, UK: Boydell Press.

Bate, Keith, ed. (1976). *Three Latin Comedies*. Toronto, Cantre for Medieval Studies.

Burns, E. Jane (1985), *Arthurian Fictions: Re-reading the Vulgate Cycle*, Columbus: Ohio State University Press.

Carley, J. P. (1984), "Polydore Vergil and John Leland on King Arthur: The Battle of the Books", *Interpretations* (15): 86–100.

Chaney, Edward (1998). *The Evolution of the Grand Tour: Anglo-Italian Cultural Relations Since the Renaissance*. London: Frank Cass.

Chatzipanagioti-Sangmeister, Julia (2006) (in German). *Griechenland, Zypern, Balkan und Levante: eine kommentierte Bibliographie der Reiseliteratur des 18. Jahrhunderts*. Eutin: Lumpeter and Lasel.

Cohen, Robert. (2000). *Theatre: Brife Edition*. Mayfield Publishing Company, p. 201-203.

Dumville, D. N. (1977), "Sub-Roman Britain: History and Legend", *History* 62 (62): 173–92.

Evans, D. Simon (1986), *Medieval religious literature*. Writers of Wales series. Cardiff : University of Wales Press.

Forbush, William Byron; Forbush, Dascomb (1915), , The Camelot Project at the University of Rochester, retrieved 2008-05-22.

Gilbert, Adrian; Wilson, Alan; Blackett, Baram (1998), *The Holy Kingdom*, London: Corgi.

Green, Thomas (1998), Ashe, Geoffrey (1985), *The Discovery of King Arthur*, Garden City, NY: Anchor Press/Doubleday.

Haycock, M. (2007), *Legendary Poems from the Book of Taliesin*, Aberystwyth: CMCS.

Higham, N. J. (2002), *King Arthur, Myth-Making and History*, London: Routledge.

Jarman, A. O. H. (1981), *The Cynfeirdd : early Welsh poets and poetry.* Writers of Wales series. Cardiff : University of Wales Press.

Jones, Gwyn; Jones, Thomas, eds. (1949), *The Mabinogion*, London: Dent.

Koch, John T. (1996), "The Celtic Lands", in Lacy, Norris J., *Medieval Arthurian Literature: A Guide to Recent Research*, New York: Garland, pp. 239–322.

Lacy, Norris J. (1992–96), *Lancelot-Grail: The Old French Arthurian Vulgate and Post-Vulgate in Translation*, New York: Garland. 5 vols.

Littleton, C. Scott; Malcor, Linda A. (1994), *From Scythia to Camelot: A Radical Reassessment of the Legends of King Arthur, the Knights of the Round Table and the Holy Grail*, New York: Garland

McKenna, Catherine A. (Ed.) (1991), *The medieval Welsh religious lyric : poems of the Gogynfeirdd, 1137-1282*. Belmont : Ford & Baillie.

Nelson, Alan H. (1972) "Some Configurations of Staging in Medieval English Drama" *Medieval English Drama: Essays Critical and Contextual* University of Chicago Press, p.116-147.

Speake, Jennifer (2003). *Literature of Travel and Exploration: An Encyclopedia*. New York: Fitzroy Dearborn.

Stephen A. Barney (1989). "Allegory". *Dictionary of the Middle Ages.* vol-1

Sylvia Huot. *Allegorical Play in the Old French Motet*. Stanford, 1997.

Symes, Carol, (2007). A Common Stage: Theatre and Public Life in Medieval Arras, Cornell University Press.

Walsh, Martin. (2002). "Drama." *Medieval Folklore: A Guide to Myths, Legends, Tales, Beliefs, and Custons. Oxford University Press, p. 103-107.*

Index